The
Future of
Food Business

The **FACTS**→The **IMPACTS**→The **ACTS**

Marcos Fava Neves
University of Sao Paulo, Brazil

World Scientific

NEW JERSEY · LONDON · SINGAPORE · BEIJING · SHANGHAI · HONG KONG · TAIPEI · CHENNAI

Published by

World Scientific Publishing Co. Pte. Ltd.

5 Toh Tuck Link, Singapore 596224

USA office: 27 Warren Street, Suite 401-402, Hackensack, NJ 07601

UK office: 57 Shelton Street, Covent Garden, London WC2H 9HE

British Library Cataloguing-in-Publication Data
A catalogue record for this book is available from the British Library.

THE FUTURE OF FOOD BUSINESS
The Facts, The Impacts and The Acts

ISBN-13 978-981-4365-83-3 (pbk)
ISBN-10 981-4365-83-1 (pbk)

Typeset by Stallion Press
Email: enquiries@stallionpress.com

Printed in Singapore.

The
Future of
Food Business

The F**ACTS**→The IMP**ACTS**→The **ACTS**

FOREWORD

When we consider the future of food, there are certainly more questions than answers because the subject of food is both complex and controversial. Discussions about food — including the social, economic and environmental impacts — seem to be happening everywhere today, from the classrooms of the most elite academic institutions to developing countries where people are rioting due to a lack of food security.

Many pertinent questions, demanding responses, are weighing on the food industry and the world.

- How will we meet the food demand of our growing population?
- What are the "best practices" for agriculture and food production?
- How do we increase the nutritional value of calories consumed to achieve a higher quality of life for people belonging to different socioeconomic strata?

It is important to note that the answers to the questions that challenge the food industry — from the laboratory to the supermarket — cannot be viewed from a single perspective. Bearing this in mind, there are different platforms which can have a real and positive impact on the future of food. Some of these are:

- Creative partnerships through which organizations combine resources of infrastructure and human capital to make exponential impacts

- Innovation frameworks based on openness, transparency and viewed from a global perspective
- Global knowledge sharing models which transfer best practices in a locally-relevant manner

I commend Marcos for boldly addressing 'The Future of the Food Business' and for the spirit of collaboration with which he approached this project.

The future is hopeful. We are living in a time when the world is more connected as never before. Innovations and scientific discoveries around the world are continuously offering new solutions to "fill the gap" of the world's demand for food. As a society, we need to have a strong sense of clarity as to "what" we must accomplish in this regard. Our responsibility, as we move forward, is to work on "how" this needs to be done.

We at Novus, in pursuit of our Vision "to help feed the world wholesome and affordable food", commit ourselves to Marcos's challenge everyday and we hope that after reading this book you will join us in doing so.

Thad Simons
President and CEO
Novus International, Inc.

CONTENTS

ACKNOWLEDGEMENTS

I would like to thank Novus International, Inc., Missouri, US, for their support in publishing this book which is a collection of my papers published in leading newspapers around the world . I would also like to thank the following organizations: Markestrat, School of Economics and Business (FEARP), Fundace and the University of Sao Paulo for their unflinching support.

Part 1

THE FOOD PRODUCTION CHAINS ENVIRONMENT

....

Chapter 1

FROM FARMS TO ... EVERYTHING[1]

This chapter provides insights into what is happening with our farms and farmers. From a traditional perspective, technology and other advancements made farms a multi-product and service supplier. I can immediately think of 13 industries whose products come from farms and we are not aware of it.

From Farm to Food and Beverages (1): this is a well known function of a farm — produce food, including grains, fruits, eggs, vegetables, juices, milk, beef, fibers and others for a growing and a richer population that demands quantity, quality, procedures, conservation, environment, animal welfare and others.

From Farm to Feed (2): a traditional industry benefiting from farms — supplies food for growth and development of animals, involving nutrition of large-sized animals, for pets etc. Part of the money spent in pet shops goes to farms.

From Farm to Fuel (3): several countries initiated biofuels blending programs, which means fuel coming from a farm using corn, wheat, sugar beet, grasses, residues and sources like sugar cane that have been used for a long time. When someone fills up the fuel tank in New York, part of the money (10%) spent on it is directed to farms, since 10% of the fuel is corn ethanol added to gasoline.

From Farm to Pharma-Medicine (4): a growing segment called "nutra-ceuticals" which means blending food together with medicine. Products with nutrients like juice with calcium,

[1] Published in *China Daily*, 13/01/2011, page 9.

lycopene, vitamins, proteins, omegas, and several other merged products are used to produce "nutra-ceuticals".

From Farm to Pharma-Cosmetics (5): a growing segment called "nutri-cosmetics" i.e. products that contain contains nutrients that enhance beauty, skin, tanning, and other characteristics desired by consumers are used to produce "nutri-cosmetics".

From Farm to Electricity (6): several farm products are used as renewable sources of electricity, for e.g., burning the farm products, e.g. sugarcane, in boilers and generating heat that is transformed into electricity, and sold.

From Farm to Plastics (7): several companies are now planning to substitute plastic originating from oil with renewable plastic coming from green and farm materials. Coca Cola recently launched its plant-based bottle that is manufactured from cane.

From Farm to Environment (8): farms play an important role in global warming, afforestation, reviving creeks surroundings, rivers, and carbon credit markets.

From Farm to Entertainment/tourism (9): for the past few years, farms have been extensively promoted as places to spend weekends, celebrate festivals and family events, and for educational purposes where in kids from schools visit farms and learn new things.

From Farm to Textiles and Clothing Industry (10): natural fibers used to produce textiles and clothes originate from cot-ton farms. Natural fibers are also used to produce hats.

From Farm to Shoe and Leather Industry (11): leather comes from cattle and other animals, which are raised and taken care of in farms.

From Farm to Construction and Furniture (12): majority of wood used to build walls, roofs and to make furniture comes from pinus, eucalyptus, compensated woods and other sources.

From Farm to Paper (13): paper is manufactured from processed farmed wood pulp. We should be thankful to farmers as we use papers and pencils in our everyday life.

Figure 1:   13 Points — From Farms To ... Everything

Source: Author.

I have summarized at least 13 industries whose products comes from farmers and consequently benefit from existence of farmers. Surprising!!!!

So let us respect our farmers. Their presence can be felt in our day-to-day lives more than what we can imagine.

Chapter 2

NAVIGATING THE GLOBAL FOOD SYSTEM[2]

In June 2010, the 20th Conference of the International Food and Agribusiness Management Association (IFAMA, www.ifama.org) was held in the beautiful city of Boston. Around 300 food and agribusiness experts and managers came together to discuss about the global food system in the new era. Established in 1990, IFAMA serves as a forum for discussion of the future of food and agribusiness and hosts an annual event in this regard. Companies like Sysco, Coca-Cola, Los Grobo, Novus, British Foods, Fonterra, Alltech, Cofco, Rabobank and GlobalGap participated in the 2010 Conference.

One of the most important topics discussed was the macro-environmental trend of increase in food consumption. Asia is creating a huge middle-class income population, with the possibility of almost one billion people moving towards the middle class. All the forecasts made ten years ago in terms of production, exports and imports for China/Asia were incomplete, and some of these were very inaccurate. Soybean imports today are much more that what was projected for 2030. When asked, a COFCO/China executive and presenter did not wish to give projection even for 2020. Rabobank predicts a 109% growth in food consumption ten years from now. Today, if China intends to be self sufficient in producing soybeans, over 35 million new

---

[2] Published in *China Daily*, 25/06/2010, page 9.

THE FUTURE OF FOOD BUSINESS

hectares should be dedicated to raise the crop. But the country does face shortage of land in this regard. Importing soybeans into China also requires importing fresh water. Overexploitation of water resources is already creating problems in China and India. Half of the world's population is located in less than a third of the arable land, and this means an increased trading of food in the future. We will need bigger ships, bigger ports and more efficient logistics and transport systems.

The dilemma of having to use the same land to produce food, fiber, feed and fuel was also discussed. In a global perspective, about 10% of grains in the world is used to produce fuel (biodiesel), 35% of the USA's corn to produce ethanol and 50% of Brazilian sugarcane to produce fuel.

The good news is that agriculture is capable of coping with different trends in food consumption and biofuels. In the past 40 years, food production has doubled and may continue to increase, since farming is going global with faster land deals in countries that are cost-efficient. For a Singapore-based company like Olam and for other similar sourcing and trading companies based elsewhere in the world, supply chain arbitrages to produce cheaper and better products is the way forward. Therefore, they make huge investments on the supply side in several countries. The case of CHS (a large cooperative in the US), which serves as a lesson to other cooperatives, was also discussed. CHS does not produce in US anymore and produces in Brazil instead. It is looking at expanding its production in the next 10 years and looking for land in different parts of the world. Farmers and cooperatives will go global and South America (well ahead of Africa) will be next food frontier to be conquered, although it lacks investment in logistics.

The definition of agribusiness in 1955 was quite simple, since in the past, most societies were mostly dedicated to agriculture.

8

Changing food system — from commodity companies to consumer companies — has made it difficult to re-define agribusiness in the recent times. Food has become a culture, economic development and a new integrated partnership system in itself. Many health insurance companies around the world are working together with food companies, since food is the most important element of health.

There is a thin line between private companies, public companies and NGOs, and this is enabling people to avoid conflict of interests. How do we know that what we are doing is good? Third party evaluators, who will be able to answer this question, will become the fastest growing industry in the food business.

There is an immediate need to create managers who can look at the totality of these decisions, since food production, health, nutrition, environment, climate control are not isolated public policy issues. We need to approach these issues from a in a multidisciplinary point of view and not treat multifaceted problems as isolated. We are living in a new world of multidisciplinarity which is very complex and ever-changing.

Chapter 3

THE ROOTS OF FOOD AND AGRIBUSINESS THINKING[3]

January was a historical month for the Harvard Business School. The traditional Cases Seminar completed 50 years of existence. Every year, around 200 executives from different parts of the world come together to discuss 12 cases of companies that share their experiences that help us contribute towards a more efficient and sustainable world.

The Seminar also has interesting dynamics. Each case is written by a team of Harvard professors and researchers. A traditional case extends over 20 pages with ten pages of text and another ten pages of annexes (financial and market data). Each case reports historical facts of each company, and focuses on its future challenges and decisions.

In a case discussion event, like the Harvard Seminar, each participant has access to the HBS web, downloads the cases, materials and instructions, and has to read the case in advance. At the Seminar, each case is than initially discussed with a smaller group of 8 participants, to create a more interactive opinion building process. Then, the case is finally discussed at a plenary meeting, and finally, the CEO of the company answers questions, and interacts with the audience. It is a four-day event in which all participants are fully engaged. If the participants do not read the cases in advance, they may find it difficult to participate in discussions.

---

[3] Published in *China Daily*, 26/01/2010, page 9.

The term "agribusiness" was discussed in length at Harvard in 1957. The concept was an attempt to bring about more integration, considering agriculture as an activity strongly linked with suppliers of inputs, service providers, the processing industry, distribution systems, financial institutions and consumers. In 1968, the new concept of "agribusiness systems" was introduced. The difference here is that an agribusiness system considers the flow of one product over an interactive system or food chain. The sum of all the systems operating in a particular country represents the country's agribusiness.

In the 2010 Seminar, 12 cases were discussed. Usually, at least one case will be focus on China and about 10 executives from China participate in the discussion. In 2009, the COFCO case was written, presented and discussed. In 2010, the DaChan Food Company was in the spotlight. This case presented the description of the company, its origins, the operations on feed, meat, how the company contracts farmers in an integrated system of producers, and the most important point was how DaChan developed a reliable system of transparency and traceability to guarantee quality for its buyers. DaChan became a major supplier for international foodservice chains operating in Asia.

Another case study focused on Cosan, the largest ethanol company in Brazil, and its recent growth strategies. This case discussed the outstanding results that Brazil has attained with ethanol, which will be discussed later in the book. Yet another case on Monsanto explored the position of the company in innovation, acquiring seed companies as "transporters of technology" to farmers, and changing communication strategies and adoption of new trends followed by farmers. The innovation pipeline that was discussed seemed to suggest that in future there will be more plants resistant to water scarcity. The Woolf case explored the production of horticulture and almonds in California, and how water restrictions are threatening future production.

The case of Rabobank, the largest cooperative bank based in the Netherlands, was also explored. The unique characteristics and the future growth strategies of the Bank, with a focus on food and agribusiness systems was discussed. Another case on Purecircle explored the market for stevia-based sugar, a natural sweetener. The cases of Ebro Puleva, the world's largest rice company based in Spain, and Hungerit, which explored poultry production in Hungary before and after the communist era, were also discussed.

An interesting case was that of GTC Biotherapeutics, a company that produces medicine and food, providing ingredients, proteins and other medicines made from food and animals. Other cases that were discussed were:

— Red Tomato, a company that links local food producers to supermarkets.
— Diamond Foods, which started as a farmers' cooperative and is now a leading company in the almond snacks market in the USA, with farmers as shareholders of the company.
— Codevasf, a public company in Brazil that is lending 8,000 ha of irrigated land to the private sector in a very interesting bid that considers sustainable integration. This case was written by us.

Chapter 4

THE GLOBAL FOOD CONSUMER[4]

There is a failure in the introduction of new products, for several reasons. Research done in the USA, with 11,000 products launched by 77 companies, discovered that only 56% of the products survived five years after they were introduced. It is interested to note how few companies that do not offer good service, do not care for consumers and ignore information and insights that consumers bring with them, manage to survive. However, such companies cannot survive in the long run. Why is it important to understand consumer behavior?

It is important to understand consumer behavior to be more capable to predict, with higher chance of being correct, and to discover cause-and-effect relationships to product's purchase and also to comprehend how the education process of this consumer is during his relationship with the company. It starts with the Buying Behavior Model analysis. The consumers' buying decision process is influenced by (i) the marketing stimulus that is caused by product characteristics, price, place and promotion strategies (ii) external environment stimulus that is caused due to economical, political, social and cultural aspects of the environment (Figure 2).

The Consumer's Buying Decision Process shown in Table 1 can be analyzed in a more detailed manner. Attempts are being made to discover tools that may be used for the food companies and develop structured market research to identify the

---

[4] Published in *China Daily*, 06/04/2010, page 9.

Figure 2: Buying Behavior Model

Source: Philip Kotler.

preferences of consumers and deliver goods to them accordingly. Table 1 shows the consumer buying decision process.

Of late, food and beverage companies have been facing important challenges that result from changes in the preferences of the end consumer. The goal of this chapter is to point out the many changes in the preferences of food consumers worldwide and show companies certain attributes of this trend that may be useful in developing new products and improve their communication with consumers, such as messages for advertising, sales promotion, and so on. I will highlight these preferences using the trends in an alphabetical order.

Authenticity and Ageing: Be authentic, recognizing mistakes with honesty and respecting the consumer (in recalls). Much attention should be paid to the ageing consumer.

Beauty: Companies need to care about the appearance of the food, work hard at the sales venue, and focus on attractive packaging of products, since more than 70% of decisions are made at the point of sale.

Convenience and Citizenship: Products need easy handling and attractive packages. The distribution channels must be chosen kpeeing in view fast and easy purchase. It is also important to focus on social actions establish a closer contact with the local community.

Table 1: Consumers' Buying Decision Process

Stage of the Process	How Does It Happen?	How Can Companies Use It?	Which Questions Can Be Formulated for the Consumers?
Buying Needs Identification	Personal values and needs associated to the external influences, (mainly originated from social interaction) make the current situation different from the desired situation, thus a *need* appears.	Apply the most frequent and efficient stimulus to stimulate this need , for example, advertising showing benefits of healthy products, or simply tasty products. The package must communicate these values, acting as a "mini out-door".	• Which need is satisfied by consuming this product? • Are these needs evident? • To what extent are the target consumers involved in the product?
Information Search	The search is done through internal sources (memory, knowledge) and external sources (market and personal relations).	Identify how much the consumer searches for information and through which sources. This helps the company to better design the price, distribution and mainly the communication plan strategies. The company must work on the sources that mostly influence consumers.	• Which product or brand does the consumer have in mind? • Is the consumer motivated to search external sources? What are those sources? • Which are the most searched attributes?

(Continued)

17

Table 1: *(Continued)*

Stage of the Process	How Does It Happen?	How Can Companies Use It?	Which Questions Can Be Formulated for the Consumers?
Alternatives Evaluation	The consumer will choose the alternative which is the strongest on the criteria that he or she values the most.	• The company must identify, through research, which product's attributes the consumer values the most, and it has to be strongly competitive in these attributes. • Repositioning attributes, repositioning competitors, changing also the analysis of the attributes (as per importance of each).	• Does the consumer evaluate and compare the alternatives? • Which are the alternatives and the what is the criteria of their choice? Can these be changed? • What is the result of the evaluation of alternatives? • Are the alternatives really different? Can the consumer prove that?
Buying Decision	Decisions are made based on the purchase itself, where to buy, when to buy, and what to buy and, finally, how to pay.	• Maximum effort should be put in at the sales venue (2/3 of the buying decision for food and beverage is made at point of sale). • Pay attention to the growth of purchases via alternative channels, like mail, email, webs, telephone and catalogues.	• Will the consumer spend time and energy till he or she finds the best alternative? • Where does the consumer prefer to buy the product (channel) and at what moment of his or her day?

(Continued)

Table 1: *(Continued)*

Stage of the Process	How Does It Happen?	How Can Companies Use It?	Which Questions Can Be Formulated for the Consumers?
After-buying behavior	Comparison between the expectations and the performance of the product. The consequences range from extreme satisfaction and positive word-of-mouth to legal attitudes towards the company.	• Have a 0800 line or an email that works efficiently. • Have researchers monitor consumer satisfaction. • Remember that only 5% of the unsatisfied consumers complain. The others simply will never buy again.	• Is the consumer satisfied with the product or service? • What are the reasons for this satisfaction/ dissatisfaction? Does he/she discuss this with other people? • Is there any intention of repeating the purchase? If yes, why?

Source: Author.

Diversity: Consumers look for a range of alternatives within the brand for each market segment. These must be attractive, with colored, different, funny and mainly educative products.

Exotic and Environment: Meals from different origins (countries, regions of the country) with exotic characteristics. This is linked to the desire for fun during mealtimes. There is also a valorization of the environment, creating opportunities for actions of sustainability, and products with a stamp of environmental preservation.

Functional Foods: Add to the products functional characteristics, such as weight reducers and energizers, and also medical characteristics, working together with medicine and health researchers. "The food will be the medicine".

Guarantee: Companies must honor their commitments to the consumer.

Harmony and Health: Consumers want equilibrium in the communication, price, products and distribution channel actions of a company. Think in terms of products with lower levels of sugar or cholesterol, and healthy products. There is an opportunity here for products in the fitness line.

Innovation and Individualization: Intensify the launch of innovative products and ideas really representing new solutions. There is also a trend towards individual products, smaller packages, for consumers who live alone.

Jobs: Products that can generate jobs, with brands and stamps for small producers, or "job friendly products".

Labeling: There are several opportunities to label products, as a very important source of information.

Meal Solutions: Offer real solutions to final consumer's desires. The food-service is getting bigger. More and more people go out for dinner or fast-foods.

Nostalgia: There is also a movement towards bringing back special moments from the past. We see an increase in old fashioned, or "retro" designed products and packages.

Organic: Products that refer to a clean environment or a controlled growth process have a growing market.

Practical and Price: Practical products for day-to-day use, quick to prepare and easy to use. Price is fundamental in the moment of decision.

Quality: Quality is a basic requisite for operating in any market. Consumers have information and the media is pressuring companies towards quality controls.

Reliable: The origins, the sources, the methods of preparation have to be reliable in the consumer's mind.

Services: There are always opportunities to offer services to consumer that really add value for the company and the consumer.

Tradition and Traceability: One company has to evaluate carefully the maintenance of its tradition in product line. Use arguments of age and time in the market, transmitting trust. Register all products' history, from the farm to the final consumer. Then, it's necessary to communicate this action mainly on clear packages for reading.

Uniformity: The consumer is not willing to accept variations in the product, especially those which a company claims to be standardized.

Table 2: Resume of the "ABC of the Food Consumer"

Attributes	The Opportunities to the Companies
A — Authenticity and Aging	— Care in the launch of new products, following the needs of the target market. — Be authentic, recognizing mistakes and with honesty and respecting the consumer (in recalls). — Care to the ageing consumer.
B — Beauty	— Care about the appearance of the food. — Work hard at the sales place. — Beautiful packages.
C — Convenient and Citizenship	— Products of easy handling and practical packages. — The distribution channels must be chosen for the fast and easy purchase. — Social actions creating a closer contact with the community.
D — Diversity	— Diverse options within a product line and the range of alternatives within the brand. — Attract with colored, different, funny and mainly educative products. — The consumers want to have fun and knowledge (information) during their meals.
E — Exotic and Environment	— Meals from different origins (countries, regions of the country, etc) with exotic characteristics. This is linked to the desire of fun during the meals. — Gradual valorization of the environment, creating opportunities for actions of sustainability. — Products with stamp of environmental preservation. (Ex: ISO 14000).
F — Functional	— Add to the products functional characteristics as weight reducers and energizers. — "The food will be the medicine".
G — Guarantee	— Honor the commitments with the consumer, like recalls, or aspects related to quality or safety.
H — Harmony and Healthy	— Equilibrium of the communication, price, products and distribution channels actions. — Products with lower level of sugar or cholesterol, healthy products. There is an opportunity here for products of the fitness line.

(Continued)

Table 2: (*Continued*)

Attributes	The Opportunities to the Companies
I — Innovation and Individualization	— Intensify the launch of new products; innovative products, really representing new solutions. — Individual products, smaller packages, to consumers that live alone.
J — Jobs	— Products that can generate jobs, with brands and stamps for small producers, or "job friendly product".
L — Labeling	— Several opportunities to label products, and the label as a very important source of information.
M — Meal Solutions	— Offer real solutions to final consumer's desires. The food-service is getting bigger. More and more people have gone out for dinner or fast-food.
N — Nostalgic	— As opposite, offer products that bring back special moments from the past of a generation that compose the target- market.
O — Organic	— Organic products. Products that refer to a clean environment.
P — Practical and Price	— Practical products for the day-to-day, with quick prepare and easy to open. — Variable price is fundamental in the decision's moment.
Q — Quality	— Basic requisite to operate in any market.
R — Reliable	— The food quality, sources, way of prepare have to be reliable in the consumer's mind.
S — Services	— Offer services to consumer. Services that really add value.
T — Tradition and Traceability	— One company has to evaluate carefully the maintenance of its traditional product line. — Use arguments of age and time in the market transmitting trust. — Register all the product's history, from the farm to the final consumer. Then, it's necessary to communicate this action mainly on clear packages for reading.

(*Continued*)

Table 2: (*Continued*)

Attributes	The Opportunities to the Companies
U — Uniformity	— Consumer is not willing to accept variations in the product, mainly those which accompany to be standardized.
V — Value	— Add value to the food, at the lowest cost, bringing the concept of "best value", used frequently in the USA.
W — World-Wide	— Explore the global food consumer that likes to recognize the food wherever in the planet he or she is.
X — Xenophobia	— Present in some countries, linked to the question of the valorization of the domestic jobs and domestic production.
Y — Young	— Some consumers want to be and to feel young, to live more, to live healthier.
Z — Zzzzz (Speed)	— The company cannot be slow. Speed is fundamental. Search on web pages, copy if necessary, have new ideas, be alert to the new opportunities, be always ahead of competitors, surprise them and the consumers.

Source: Author.

Value Proposition: Add value to the food, at the lowest cost, bringing in the concept of "best value" in the category.

World-Wide: Explore the global food consumer, who likes to recognize the food wherever on the planet he or she is, linked to the open and global communications platform.

Xenophobia: Present in some countries, and linked to the question of the valorization of domestic jobs and domestic production.

Young: There is the forever young movement; some consumers want to be and to feel young, to live longer, to live more healthily.

Zzzzz — (Speed): Companies cannot be slow. Speed is fundamental. Search on web pages, copy if necessary, have new ideas, be alert to new opportunities, always be ahead of competitors, surprise them and the consumers.

Companies could consider: what opportunities do you see in the future? What arguments, within those listed, do you have? How to use those arguments in a very positive way? Does the consumer identify and value this argument in his or her buying decision process? Which of those arguments can be adapted? In summary, I have tried to bring ideas, arguments, messages to enable the food and beverage companies to offer products that have consequently more value and acceptance.

Chapter 5

THE WORLD OF RETAILER BRANDS[5]

Private labels (brands developed and managed by distributors, retailers and wholesalers) are currently one of the most discussed issues of strategy and have a major impact on retailers' activities. They have been important tools for distributors in a very competitive sector and have been both threats and opportunities to the food industry. The objective of this article is to select some important aspects to be considered in relation to supplying food products under a retail or wholesale distributor's private label.

In some countries, the share of private labels in the retail market has reached over 50% of total food sales. Some retailers sell only their own brand in their stores. The percentage of private label sales in the food and beverages industry is higher than of other product categories. But what are the possible advantages for food producers when they decide to sell their products to private labels?

There are several possible advantages. Firstly, since communication is done by the retailer, this represents lower costs for the producer. There is also a possibility of increasing sales and obtaining gains from economies of scale, since the producer will occupy a higher percentage of both factory capacity and the volume of inputs bought, thus increasing their power to negotiate with suppliers. The producer can also occupy a larger space on the retailers' shelves (this happens when there are two brands from the same factory — the original and the private label).

[5] Published in *China Daily*, 20/04/2010, page 9.

For a food producer, it could also be easier to obtain credit and funding from banks, since future sales are guaranteed by supply contracts. In product line decisions, it gives the possibility of switching to alternative product lines with different prices and positioning. It is important to note that these are normally products that are not at the forefront of technological innovation, since hardly any new products are launched as private labels. There is an improvement in the relationship with the retailer. An advantage for food companies is reputation, since consumers recognize that being a supplier of a retailer is considered to be a certification of quality. It may also possibly reduce physical distribution costs, since food producers do not need promoters at the point of sale.

Another point that should be considered is that the company's main brand may face a drop in the market share, but the factory will command a higher share of the market since there are now two brands of products being produced at the factory. As the company gains experience and is able to supply other retailers and industries, there is the opportunity to become the global supplier in that category of food. One practical reason to consider this proposal is that if the company does not occupy this space on the market, competitors will only be too glad to do so.

As for the retailer, what are the advantages of having products with their brands on them? First we need to understand that there are two possible types of product: a brand with the name of the retail chain, or a retail brand, but with another name and retailer stamp on the product. There is an advantage in vertical chain coordination by having production without production assets. It will also be possible to have stock reductions since these products will be managed by the company. Given the flexibility of private labels' price positioning, the retailer's bargaining power in relation to other suppliers is also increased. This strategy adds the possibility of consumers developing brand loyalty by identifying with that brand when they see it at home or in other places.

Table 3: Points of Possible Advantage for Food Producers and Retailers in Relation to Private Labels

Possible Advantages for the Food Producer to Establish this Relationship	Possible Advantages for the Retailer to Establish this Relationship
• Communication is done by the retailer: possible lower communication (advertising/product promotion) costs for industry • Possibility to increase sales and obtain scale gains: higher occupation of factory capacity and increase purchases of factor inputs, enhancing negotiation power with suppliers • A larger space occupied on the retailer shelves (this happens when there are two brands from the same factory — the original company brand and the private label) • Possible liberation of products sold on consignment (a request usually made to the food industry by retailers) • Could be easier to obtain credit and funding by banks, since future sales are guaranteed by the private label supply contract • Product mix: possibilities of alternative product lines with different prices and positioning • Normally these are products without technological innovation. Hardly any new products are launched as private labels • Possible improvement in the relationship with the retailer, receiving better shelf space, without paying slotting allowances and other retailer taxes • Consumers and distributors recognize the company quality (being that particular retailer's supplier of the private label brand works as a quality certification) • A possible lower physical distribution cost	• Two types of possible products: brands with the name of the retail chain, and retail brands, but with another name and retailer stamp on the product. Each has its advantages and disadvantages • Vertical chain coordination allows production without production assets • Possibility of stock reductions since these products will be managed by the industry • Higher bargaining power to negotiate with other suppliers given by the flexibility of the private label's price positioning • Possibility of developing store loyalty • Possibility of higher margins • Increased competition for shelf space • Store's product line gets wider, but will require careful quality monitoring because the brand image can be damaged if there are problems

(Continued)

29

Table 3: (*Continued*)

Possible Advantages for the Food Producer to Establish this Relationship	Possible Advantages for the Retailer to Establish this Relationship
• Promoters are not needed at the point of sale • A possible lower market share for the main company's brand at the store, but a higher market share for the factory (since now it has two brands coming from the factory at the shelves) • The retailer gains experience and can also supply other retailers and industries • As the retailing sector becomes more global, there is the opportunity to be the global supplier for that category of food • If one industry does not occupy this space, a competitor will occupy it	

Source: Author.

Private labels normally offer higher margins and increase competition for shelf space: once the limited space is filled with its own products, this reduces space for other companies to share.

Another possible advantage is that the store's product line may grow wider. But the retailer needs to have very good coordination, since it has to ensure careful quality monitoring to ensure that the brand's image is not damaged by problems in the new products.

Since retailers are recognized and in some cases very admired by consumers, why not extend their brands to the products sold in the stores? Private labels today are a major issue in marketing, as they have increased the competition in the food market and enhanced retailers' bargaining power. Market leaders are threatened by increasing private label sales even within premium segments, while the second or third brands in the market are also being threatened by cheaper private labels.

Chapter 6

RETAILERS, THE GIANTS OF CHAINS[6]

In some meetings, I have seen retailers' sales forecasts for 2010. Wal-Mart, the leader, is expected to sell an amazing €337 billion worth of food from 8,400 stores across 15 countries. Carrefour is the second largest, and expected to sell €115 billion worth of food in 35 countries. The next is Tesco, far away with €78 billion of food sales. Although these numbers are impressive, since they are even higher than some countries, the market share of these retailers has decreased. In 2003 the top 20 retailers had 23.4% of market share, and in 2010 they now have around 21% of total sales in the world. Why has this happened?

We offer one possible explanation. When comparing the size of retail markets in several countries, the changes are impressive. In 2006, these countries represented the ten largest markets: USA (€612 billion), China (€328 billion), Japan (€297 billion), France (€206 billion), India (€190 billion), UK (€188 billion), Germany (€150 billion), Italy (€127 billion), Russia (€116 billion) and Mexico (€112 billion). Using recent statistics to project the figures for 2014, the ten largest markets will be China (€761 billion), USA (€745 billion), India (€448 billion), Japan (€360 billion), Russia (€322 billion), Brazil (€284 billion), France (€228 billion), UK (€198 billion), Germany (€168 billion) and Indonesia (€167 billion). The reader may note that three years from now, the BRIC countries will

---

[6] Published in *China Daily*, 07/10/2010, page 9.

comprise 4 of the 6 largest markets. In these emerging countries, one possible explanation is that the retail market has a higher concentration ratio.

Below follow some points that we should consider when analyzing food retailers.

To start the thinking process, let us consider the subject: private or retailers' labels. This is definitely one of the most important points. Their percentage share of food sales is increasing, and in some chains, mostly in Germany, they may have 60 or 70% of the market share. In Switzerland, 47% of the market has been conquered by private labels. Several other European countries have retailers occupying more than 30% of the market share. Private labels in Brazil, India, China and Russia still have less than 10% of the market share, so we may expect several changes in the future.

Another point that is probably linked to the decline of the concentration ratio in the retail market is the trend towards neighborhood concepts centered around greater convenience and proximity. Retailers have a multi-format system in place, comprising first hypermarkets and supermarkets, then members' clubs and convenience and discount stores. But the number of neighborhood stores is increasing due to trends among consumers who buy smaller quantities at more frequent intervals.

Information and communications with consumers, since retailers dominate two valuable assets: information about consumers (what, who, when, why they buy) and space for interactions and selling. Retailers are selling this information to food companies and are willing to offer more for space for food industry communications inside stores, since these represent a growing source of income. For the industry, since almost 70% of buying decisions are made at the points of sale, this strategy represents an opportunity to decisively influence the consumer's preference.

Table 4: Questions for Food Retailers — The Giants

	Questions	List Ideas and Opportunities for the Company
Private or retailers' labels	— What changes can we expect in the area of private and/or retailers' labels?	
Trend towards neighborhood concept	— Why are the numbers of neighborhood stores increasing? — How do we attend to new trends of consumer demand?	
Information and communications	— How do we get the information from retailers? — What strategies can we use to gain the customer's preference? — What kind of communication should we use at a point of sale?	
Challenges in operations management	— How do we reduce transaction costs? — How do we maximize shelf space?	
Services towards convenience	— How do we offer more convenient services?	
"Green movement"	— How do we save energy and measure carbon emissions?	
Strategy of sustainable sourcing	— How do we include smallholders, such as suppliers?	
Internationalization and global sourcing	— How do we face the challenge of cultural differences? — How do we find the best sources from all over the globe?	
Competition from different forms of food provision	— How do we face competition from different forms of food provision?	
Trend towards collective operations	— How can we conduct collective operations with other retailers?	

Source: Author.

33

Retailers also face new challenges with regards to operations management. These include efforts to permanently reduce transactions costs, reducing the number of suppliers without increasing dependency, and technology (electronic data interchange systems). This also highlights the need for better product assortment in order to maximize shelf space.

Services that cater to increased convenience are also becoming increasingly common among retailers. These include, but are not limited to, delivery and packaging services, offering ready-to-eat meals as replacements for home-cooked food, and the increased presence of outlets such as bakeries, butcheries and coffee shops. A trend is developing among retailers towards a "green movement" that aims to save energy and limit carbon emissions in a bid to be environmentally friendly. Not only do they adopt a policy of sustainable sourcing by using fair trade concepts and an increased inclusion of smallholders such as suppliers, but some go even further to achieve this by allowing their transaction costs to rise.

Due to internationalization and the ability to source from the entire globe, retailers face the challenge of adapting to different cultures. However, this also allows retailers to find the best suppliers from all over the globe and bring these products into their stores. Retailers also face stronger competition from other forms of food provision such as direct sales, online sales, door-to-door distribution systems, and an increasing number of "food services" such as restaurants and caterers.

Last but not least is a trend towards collective operations with other retailers, with shared purchases of necessary structures, stock management, marketing, layout, and technology sharing, which maybe a first step towards a future merger of the giants.

These are the ten topics of discussions involving the giants of the food chain. What may be useful here is to discuss these issues more deeply in order to create opportunities for these retailers.

Chapter 7

THE FOUR Ps OF SUSTAINABILITY PLANNING[7]

Sustainability in food chains is becoming increasingly important. Hence, this chapter proposes a framework that will help companies and governments to come to grips with the issue of sustainability. This framework will emphasize the importance of implementing what has been discussed. Unfortunately, in this area there is too much talk and too little action, both from governments and companies.

Sustainability, previously defined as the "responsible use of exhaustible energy resources and raw materials", has become an issue that the world is increasingly aware of. This can be seen in the rising expectations of consumers who are more aware of problems associated with sustainability, and the emergence of a new generation that is both concerned about environmental issues and that has the common sense to conserve the earth. Additionally, the increasing scarcity of the planet's natural resources, risks of global warming that will result in extensive floods leading to hunger due to the loss of agricultural land, modern communications which provide us with instant information on disasters, the environmentally unfriendly actions of companies, and excess pollution, among other issues, have all contributed to this growing awareness of sustainability.

---

[7] Published in *China Daily*, 27/11/2009, page 9.

There is growing concern among companies that in order to reduce the impact of their activities on the environment, they will have to exercise corporate social responsibility in order to promote a better flow of information, promote inclusion and reduce social imbalance, and to increase the utilization of renewable resources/energy.

Sustainability has three traditional major pillars that must be considered when promoting development. These are the economic dimension (profit), the environmental dimension (planet) and the social dimension (people). We now add a fourth "P": pro-activeness.

With regards to the economic (profit) side, the major factors to be considered are how companies, networks and production chains deal with a wide range of issues. These include profit margins, compensation, losses on the chain, communication issues for end consumers, improving credit conditions with benefits for sustainable projects, risk management, information technology, and overall strategies to reduce costs and ensure the economic sustainability of the business. Without economic sustainability, any other request is impossible, since companies cannot pay for improvements if they are not economically sustainable. This is an important first step.

With regards to the environment (planet) side, the major factors to be considered are related to the impact of the company on the environment. We must examine the behavior of the company's integrated suppliers, the extent of the use of transport, the quality and quantity of packaging, waste management policies such as recycling, the use of energy, emissions levels of both carbon and other pollutants, water management practices, the utilization of environmentally friendly buildings, and many other factors. Consumers also have a huge part to play by changing their own habits and being more responsible in their personal consumption.

With regards to the social (people) side, major factors revolve around the working conditions for the company's employees, suppliers and distributors. This includes general health and safety, the non-utilization of child labor, working climate, and the presence and utilization of safety equipment. Outside the company itself, the company should promote appropriate activites for the local community, create incentives for cooperation, possess smallholder-friendly initiatives such as offering technology transfers, improve local employment levels by increasing capacity, and promote benefits for consumers such as being concerned about nutrition and health risks.

Finally, a company must be proactive in promoting sustainability. This involves instituting a code of conduct and following the regulations of industry associations. As for governments, they should endeavor to promote awareness of sustainability, set aside a budget for such activities, initiate immediate steps

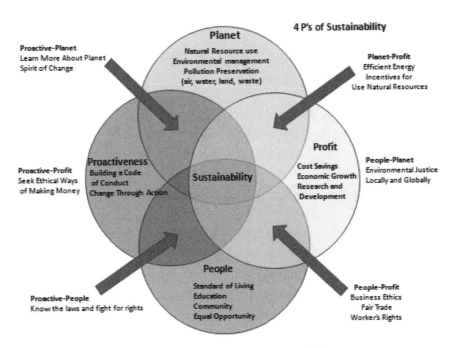

Figure 3: The Four Ps of Sustainability

Source: Author.

to reduce environmental damage by constantly monitoring economic activities for pollution and malpractices, and document, review and exchange information through committees.

A planet that is environmentally imbalanced will not be sustainable in the long term. It is our responsibility to promote better conditions for future generations to live on an earth that is in a state of environmental equilibrium. The choice is upon us. We can choose to be remembered as the generation that took action to solve these issues and save our planet, or we can choose to be known as the generation that stood back, did nothing, and watched our planet's environment go to ruin.

Chapter 8

THE GLOBAL FINANCIAL CRISIS, BRIC AND FOOD COMPANIES[8]

The economic crisis of 2008/2009 was the crisis of the 3 Cs — credit, consumption and confidence. Let us examine each in detail. Over the few years prior to the crisis, financial institutions in several countries lent credit to consumers in an irresponsible manner, creating an artificial market. It was an era of financial leverage, financial strategy, and financial dominance. Several companies entered the market, building up very risky positions by paying salaries and dividends that were out of touch with reality while neglecting costs. This initial "festival" in the financial market eventually caused a severe "hangover".

In several countries, irresponsible consumption contributed to the crisis. The abundant amounts of credit on offer led large numbers of consumers to buy what they could not otherwise afford, taking loans for houses, cars, equipment and other big ticket purchases. It was clear that this consumption was beyond the means of many household budgets, but such irresponsible consumption fueled by borrowing continued. Following the crisis, as asset prices went down, many households had no choice but to reduce leverage and sell what they had bought.

In terms of confidence, trouble with the credit and consumer markets has made society lose confidence in the system, in companies, and in governments. Since economic recovery is

---

[8] Published in *China Daily*, 12/08/2009, page 9.

related to confidence in the economy, recovery will be difficult in many countries. Due to the crisis, when uncertainty abounded, many consumers who could still consume within their means lost confidence and stopped consuming. With lower sales, markets were reduced, employment was reduced, and this lead to lower consumption, lower sales and increased unemployment with a negative cyclic effect, thus compounding the crisis. The rate of "confidence recovery" will be the key factor in determining when and how the economy will recover after the crisis. The economic situation will improve before the financial situation, since it is not yet known what is still to come in terms of bad credit. However, risks of a total financial collapse have been mitigated.

In 2009 there was also increasing political instability, i.e., governments with wrong political and economic measures, countries filing for bankruptcy, governments being deposed, and an increasing threat of instability due to military threats such as arms races and nuclear weapons tests. The uncertainty created also affected markets and consumer confidence, which make up part of the environment in which food chains operate.

It is very important to know that the 2009 world crisis cannot be generalized. It had different impacts on various individual regions, countries and industries. For example, the food, car and housing industries in Brazil experienced a record level of sales, while other industries, like heavy equipment, suffered their worst crisis in 20 years. Some countries suffered more (Germany, with a 5% decrease in GDP) and some less (China, with a 6% increase). The USA will still suffer due to the high leverage of its consumers, while predictions for European recovery are more pessimistic than those for the Americas and Asia.

Another point that contributed to a faster recovery of the global economic situation was the enormous global shift in market power. Goldman Sachs predicts that the BRIC (Brazil, Russia, India and China) group will have a higher GDP than the

G7 by 2027. Between 2000 and 2005 BRIC GDP grew from US$3.6 trillion to almost US$5 trillion. Brazil experienced an average growth rate of 3.1% per year from 2000 to 2009, and an accumulated variation of 36.3% in the same period. During this decade, China had an incredible average annual growth rate of 9.6% and an accumulated variation of 151%. India experienced an average annual growth rate of 6.9% with an accumulated variation of 94.6%, while Russia's figures were 5.5% and 71.2% respectively (FMI).

Emerging nations accounted for 11% of world GDP in 1991 and 30% in 2008. This figure is expected to reach 50% within 20 years. The world population in 2050 is expected to be 9 billion people, and only 10% of these are expected to reside in developed nations. In 2009, there were around 200 million people in emerging nations that had an annual income of US$3,000, with this number likely to grow to 2 billion people in the next 15–20 years. So there is no doubt that a huge shift has happened in the last 10 years. Diversification has taken place thanks to the entry of new consumers and markets into the global economy. This shift will be accelerated by faster technology and knowledge transfers, made possible by the development of the internet.

The GDP of large food consumers like China and India continues to grow, contributing to an increase in consumption. Goldman Sachs expects China to grow by 7–8% in 2009 and 11% in 2010, and India with 6% to 7% in 2009–2010. Almost 60% of the world's economic growth in the period 1999–2009 was in developing nations, with the BRIC countries contributing 30%.

Countries that are heavily dependent on the US for imports, tourism and remittances are suffering more that the traditional food and commodity producers and exporters, examples of the latter being Brazil, Uruguay, Colombia and Argentina. Brazil is well known as a large food and biofuels exporter. Since food is a basic necessity that will be the last thing to be cut

41

Credit	• Credit Given in an irresponsible way
Consumption	• Irresponsible consumption done by society
Confidence	• The society loses confidence in the system

Figure 4:   The Economic Crisis — 3 Cs

Source: Author.

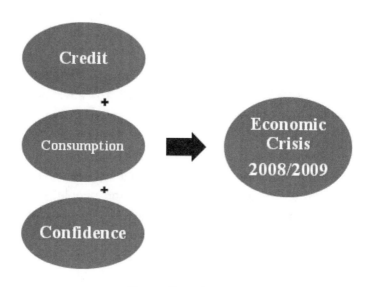

Figure 5:   The 3 Cs

Source: Author.

from a family budget, food exporters will therefore tend to have more stable incomes in times of crisis. Food demand elasticity is also low. On the other hand, markets selling higher value goods will be harder hit.

Due to several factors, Brazil is not affected by this crisis in the same way that it was in the past. Part of this is due to the Real Economic Plan, launched in 1994, which brought economic stabilization. For example, supermarket sales in April 2009 were 6.5% higher than April 2008. The economy has grown by 4–5% per year in the last few years, and although forecasts predict only 0.5–1% growth in 2009, there is agreement that it will be back to 3–4% in 2010. Goldman Sachs expects a 5% increase. The country has a small share of overall global trade, largely in the food and commodity trade, and was therefore less affected than other export driven economies. High levels of domestic consumption, tough adjustments made in the past in the banking and financial systems towards credit exposure, a high level of international currency reserves (stable at US$205 billion, while other countries like Russia, Mexico and Korea drew down on their reserves), energy security (self sufficient in oil and with more than 50% of current car fuel consumption coming from domestically produced sugarcane ethanol) and other factors contributed to this position.

To conclude this chapter, what are the messages for companies? Companies will need to focus, return to their core business, make very efficient use of capital and resources, and work even more on planning, collective action and cost structures. Companies will also need to take a very close look at risk monitoring. The current global climate requires the establishment of numerous competitive supply chains and strong value propositions for human talent. In an era of conservative leveraging and financing, companies have to take advantage of opportunities for consolidation, acquisition and merger in the world.

Chapter 9

THE FOOD CRISIS WILL BE BACK[9]

This chapter deals with the problem of food demand and the increase in food prices that arose during 2007–2008. Due to several factors, this problem is likely to recur sooner than expected.

There are nine major factors that are changing and placing pressure on the capacity to supply food to the world, and these are related to the economic and financial crisis.

Several countries are stepping up their production of biofuels, which often takes up land that should have been used for food production. Many studies link only biofuels as the cause of increasing food prices, ignoring several other factors, most of which we have been aware of for some time. Biofuels are not a major problem, since there are positive results of biofuels being produced at places that also experience increases in food production.

The projected growth of the world's population to 9 billion by 2050 is not a new factor, but it contributes to the need for increased food production. FAO/ONU estimates that the world will need to produce at least 50% more food in the next 15 years. Projections of future demand for grains (2.2 billion tons in 2009 to 3.3 billion tons in 2025), milk (3.4 billion tons in 2009 to 5 billion tons in 2017) and meat are impressive. For example, the MENA (Middle East and North African) countries have a population of around 380 million today, and are expected to have 510 million in 2025.

---

[9] Published in *China Daily*, 07/07/2009, page 9.

Economic development and income distribution in highly pop-ulated countries such as India, Brazil, Eastern Europe, China, Indonesia, Thailand, South Africa, Argentina, and the Arabian and African countries is one of the most exciting factors, bringing millions of new food consumers into the market. Several African economies have grown by more than 5% per year in the last 5–10 years. Experts in food consumption expect food expenditure increases of 50% in China, 78% in India, and 40% in developing Asia, the Middle East and North Africa within the next ten years (Global Demographics Report, 2008). From a proportion of 60%/40% consumption in developed and emerging economies, in ten years' time, the two markets will each command half of the global demand for food. China's per-centage of the world's population is more than twice the percentage of global trade attributed to China.

Stronger government programmes directed at access to food such as the one in Brazil reaching 10 million families and 40 million people continually introduce new consumers into food markets. The market for sausages in Brazil grew from US$0.5 billion in 2003 to US$1 billion in 2007. Thailand has 10 million people receiving government checks of US$58 per month. These are just some examples of events taking place in several parts of the world. Several such signs are present, but are not being captured by major economists as required.

Migration and urbanization are creating mega-cities, both causing an overall increase in food consumption as well as shift-ing consumption patterns away from grain and towards protein-based products. As such, consumption is becoming more individual-based, more sophisticated and more energy consum-ing. There is also a huge impact here, since in several countries, 50% of the population that still lives in rural areas are expected to move into the cities. A study estimates that around 350 million people in China will move into the cities by 2025. This will require 5 million buildings, which will require computers, TVs, air conditioning and new food consumption habits (equivalent of ten cities of New York).

Oil prices rose from US$35 to US$140 in five years, affecting production and transport costs. Prices are rising once more, and oil is not only used for transportation. It is also used in several other industries, like plastics, that are also experiencing increases in consumption. Even with oil prices stable at around US$70–80 a barrel, should oil prices rise again, the production of biofuels will start to become increasingly economically viable, thus increasing the demand for land at the expense of corn and other grains. China had 65 million cars running in 2008 and is expected to have 150 million by 2020, consuming 250 million tons of gas per year.

The devaluation of the US dollar in recent years has also contributed to higher commodity prices, since these are priced in US$.

Food production shortages are a result of lower profit margins, climate, droughts and diseases. This is a major concern. Due to the credit crunch and high price fluctuations, there was a downturn in prices. The criteria for borrowing credit became strict, and this together with losses of bad hedging by agribusiness companies, resulted in loss of confidence. As a consequence, due to the higher risks for planted areas and yields, hedging prices got worst due to a reduction in hedging, and consequently, there was more uncertainty and a lack of confidence in long term contracts. This may have caused reductions in productivity, running down of inventories, lower margins, and the choice by some farmers to switch to crops that are cheaper to produce. Some exporting countries will become importers. In addition, there are always concerns over the availability and costs of water, as well as the unknown future impacts of global climate change in crop productivity. This point is, therefore, a major concern.

Investment funds operating in futures markets and others in agribusiness have increased due to lower interest rates in

Table 5: The Food Crisis

9 Major Factors

1. Increase in areas dedicated for growing crops for biofuels
2. The growth of world population
3. Economic development and income distribution in populated countries
4. Stronger government programs for aid and food consumption
5. Migration and urbanization creating megacities, both increasing food consumption and changing consumption habits
6. Oil prices went up from US$35 to US$140 in five years, impacting production and transport costs
7. The dollar devaluation
8. Production shortages (Food Supply)
9. Investments funds operating in futures markets and others in agribusiness

Source: Author.

several countries. It is known that some of these have been replaced by strategic investors with conservative financing mechanisms, but there is still a movement of funds towards food commodities. This is also increasing consolidation.

Chapter 10

Strategies for Solving the Food Inflation Problem

There are two methods to solve expected food demand/inflation. Countries can choose to adopt increased protectionism, stimulate non-competitive industries to produce in an economically artificial environment and return to a policy of self-sufficiency. Alternatively, they can move towards growth, global trade and inclusion. We offer a 10-point solution to governments that can be used to combat rising food demand and inflation, which will contribute to sustainability, peace, equitable income distribution and inclusion.

Production should be expanded horizontally into new areas, bearing in mind environmental sustainability. This expansion can be done in several countries where resources are currently poorly utilized (South America uses only 25% of its capacity). In Brazil several studies confirm the existence of more than 100 million hectares of degraded pastures that can be utilized for food and biofuels production without affecting fragile ecological systems. With suitable contracts, these production and land expansions will bring about more inclusive farming, increased entrepreneurship and job creation, more equitable income distribution and economic development, and may have a positive impact on democracy. With several pension funds buying land for financial security, land prices are rising. In an example of a perfect match of investments and the need for development, a fund of US$800 million was recently established in Arabian countries. This fund is dedicated to buying land and ensuring food security, with investments being made in South American and African countries (Financial Times). China has also begun building supply chains abroad.

Production should be increased in areas that are already being utilized. This is known as vertical expansion. With improved technology, each hectare of land in developing countries can produce more food. A hectare of farmland in the US can generate two or even three times more corn than the average production per hectare in Brazil. With irrigation, some farms in the tropics can generate three crops per year. Major research and investment should be dedicated to these improvements.

Governments should work to reduce food import taxes and other trade barriers. Food prices in some countries are artificially inflated due to import taxes and other kinds of barriers that damage international trade, markets and growth. For example, beef sold by a certain retailer in the European Union costs four or five times higher than the same beef in the same retailer's Argentinean or Brazilian store. The most common argument is that lowering trade barriers will damage the local agricultural sector in less developed countries. However, it should now be assumed that the new level of commodity prices may allow local agriculture to be competitive. Several other internal taxes on food should also be reduced to lower consumer prices. This is also true for the US$330 billion spent annually by OECD members on agricultural subsidies. These subsidies put pressure on prices while undermining more cost efficient food production in naturally competitive countries.

Investment should be made in international logistics to reduce food costs. Many grain producing countries have extremely poor logistics systems. Governments and companies should work together to facilitate public-private partnerships. Ports, roads, and other food distribution and logistics systems should be privatized to increase efficiency.

Transaction costs should be reduced, since major international food chains are badly coordinated and inefficient, have several redundancies, poor use of assets, corruption and opportunism. This results in an increase in costs which affects food prices. Institutional reforms, as proposed by Douglass North, are the solution. Increasing efficiency in cooperatives, producer pools, and other collective entities will reduce redundancies and improve organization and bargaining power.

Careful consideration should be made of what crops are best used to produce biofuels in a sustainable way. Brazil is a good example. Ethanol has been produced for more than 35 years from 3.5 million hectares of cane, using only 1% of the country's arable land while supplying 52% of fuel transport requirements, with no impact on food production. The increase in both food production and biofuels in the last 10 years in the state of Sao Paulo, a major sugar cane growing region, shows that a compromise can be made. Crops with good yields that can be used for biofuels without competing with food production should be prioritized in biofuels development. The energy balance of sugar cane ethanol is 4.5 times better than that of ethanol produced from sugar beet or wheat, and almost seven times better than ethanol produced from corn (Neves *et al.*, 2009).

It is important to produce a new generation of fertilizers from plants that better absorb energy from the sun. By-products from other processes should also be recycled to mitigate the huge risk and cost of fertilizers in the future. Fertilizers are among the most important and expensive inputs for agriculture, and in times when yields must be improved, its importance becomes even greater.

Governments should provide sustainable supply contracts for farmers, with integrated sustainable investments and projects. It is of fundamental importance that margins and income should be better distributed to farmers all over the world.

Good prices are the best economic incentive for growths in production aided by technology. It is well known that the concentration of resources in several food and retailing industries retains margins that could be better distributed to farmers, thus resulting in economic development and positive externalities.

Research and investments in innovation should be stimulated from all possible sources. This should occur primarily in genetics, in order to find new genetic solutions for food and biofuels production and consumption. In trying to solve the sustainability equation, the shortage of seeds has become a problem. Public investment in agricultural research and development has decreased considerably in the past couple of decades, resulting in a yield-growth slowdown. This has disabled production and

Table 6:   The Food Demand Model

Nine Causes of Food Prices Increase	Ten Proposed Solutions
• Biofuels • Population growth • Income distribution and wealth in populated countries • Government programmes for food distribution • Urbanization and creation of mega-cities • Impact of oil prices on production and transportation costs • Production shortages due to adverse climate and financial conditions, water and climate change impacts • Dollar devaluation • Investment funds operating in commodities	• Sustainable horizontal expansion • Vertical expansion utilizing technology • Reduction in food taxes and other barriers • Investments in international logistics platforms • Use the best sources for biofuels production • Reduction of transaction costs in food chains • New generation fertilizers • Sustainable supply contracts to farmers • Innovations (genetics and others) • Consumption behavior for less energy consumption

Source: Author.

decreased the ability to keep up with rising consumption. Since society is now more trusting and accepting of biotechnology, research should receive more attention.

We must work slowly to change consumption habits in both food and fuel. Supporting 9 billion people on the planet in a sustainable manner will present several challenges. Hence, people should gradually adopt a mindset of sustainable behavior. Overconsumption of food brings about obesity, which is a major health concern. Investments need to be made in resourceful public transportation to counter inefficient consumption of fuel. While a major challenge to most countries, the city of Barcelona has implemented a public biking system which is an excellent example of a working solution.

Table 6 summarizes the causes of food price increases and proposed solutions.

Chapter 11

BRIDGING THE FOOD DILEMMA: THE CASE OF CHINA AND BRAZIL[10]

The value of trade between China and Latin American countries grew from US$10 billion in 2000 to US$140 billion in 2008. China and Brazil have strong mutual ties and a long history of peace and acceptance. The Chinese community living in Brazil is enormous and well integrated with Brazil's multiracial and multicultural society. Chinese are recognized as hard workers, having set up many businesses in the last 50 years.

China is the world's largest developing nation, where living standards have improved at the fastest rate in the world. Despite these positive developments, China will soon face problems securing adequate food supplies for its population. This is due to the rising costs of food, the increasing scarcity of clean water, changes in soil and climate conditions, and other factors. Brazil, on the other hand, has 850 million hectares of land. Of the 350 million hectares of arable land, 70 million hectares are currently being cultivated. Pastures account for another 200 million hectares, and the remaining 80 million hectares of arable land currently lie unused by farmers. In total, there exist 100 million hectares of unused land that are suitable for sustainable agriculture.

In terms of food security, the coming years are likely to see Brazil become the most important supplier of food and biofuels

---

[10] Published in *China Daily*, 31/08/2009, page 9.

to China. For example, soybean exports from Brazil to China grew by 27% from 2008 to 2009. The Brazilian share of China's imports increased from 0.7% in 2003 to almost 3% in 2009, and is expected to grow faster due to rising imports of poultry, beef and other types of food. The risks of producing food in Brazil are negligible, since the country is a large food producer and exporter. This reduces the likelihood of the government banning exports or expropriating assets, as has been seen in other countries. With such an open market, China has a safe place to produce crops to import back to the country.

Another great opportunity is to have common investments in order for Brazil to help China to address environmental concerns. Brazil has one of the cleanest energy matrices in the world. In contrast, China has problems in water supply. Of its 600 million urban inhabitants, less than 5% have access to clean air that meets European safety standards. Again we turn to the positive example of Brazil's ethanol fuel programme. 90% of all new Brazilian cars are powered by flexi fuel, while ethanol accounts for 52% of all vehicle fuel consumption in the country. By 2015, 80% of domestic demand for fuel will be for ethanol, produced from sustainable sugarcane cultivation. Only 1% of Brazil's arable land area is used to produce the fuel required to satisfy 52% of the doemstic demand for fuel. With 65% of all domestically produced emissions in China coming from automobiles, raising ethanol fuel consumption in the form of E5 and E15 fuel would cut emissions significantly. In exchange, China can offer Brazil its technology, scale and expertise in developing the latter's economy further.

Since Brazil lacks resources for investment, China may contribute in this area. The lack of good logistics and infrastructural support, especially in grain production areas, has increased the cost of commodities and food. Chinese investment would be welcome in developing roads, ports, airports, storage capacity, pipelines for ethanol, and other infrastructural projects.

Brazil is also working quickly to adapt food production towards international standards of sustainability.

It is clear that China and Brazil will work closely together in the future. Within a few years, the Chinese economy will

Table 7: "The Food Bridge Concept"

Brazil	China
• Lacks investment capacity and logistics	• Has the largest capacity for international investments and logistics
• Can rapidly expand food production	• Faces a incredible growth of income and urbanization and will need more food
• Has several possibilities for international investments	• Has a large number of investors to invest and take advantage of opportunities in Brazil
• Has low population/land availability ratio, and around 100 million hectares of land available for development	• Little new land available for food production; needs to invest abroad to guarantee food security
• World's largest exporter of beef, poultry, soybeans, juices, sugar, biofuels, coffee and in 5-10 years will be the major food exporter in most important food chains	• Scarcity of water for agriculture and climate change
• Sufficient supply of water for agriculture	• In 5-10 years will need quantities of food from abroad; most of this food will come from Brazil
• Is a net producer and exporter of the most efficient biofuel, sugarcane based ethanol, used as E100 and E25 (100% ethanol cars and 25% ethanol in gasoline)	• Will need to expand biofuels production and utilization to create a cleaner environment, such as adding biofuels to gasoline (E5 or E10). These biofuels can be produced by Chinese investments in Brazil and Africa
• Has one of the world's most diverse populations and a long-term acceptance of the Chinese community living in Brazil	• Has a large Chinese community living in Brazil
• The federal government has given great importance to relations with China	• Very good relationship on a federal level with Brazil

Source: Author.

likely be the largest in the world, making her a world leader. China and Brazil have a long history of mutual respect and admiration. The countries should immediately work on enhance future food trade to the benefit of both countries. This cooperation must include linking institutions and businesses to improve business processes and to make common investments, as well as increased joint research projects. This will help the development of a new world with environmental and human sustainability, and where differences between nations are tolerated. Table 7 summarizes the Food Bridge concept.

Chapter 12

ALTERNATIVE SOLUTIONS FOR THE FOOD CRISIS[11]

In the chapter "The Food Crisis Will Be Back", I addressed the food crisis debate. The ideas for the article came from previous research which was then further developed and published in two important academic journals.

When the article was written, food commodity prices were at comfortable levels, and I explained that the 2007-2008 crisis was a serious structural crisis caused by nine factors, each of varying levels of importance. To reiterate, they were the use of agricultural land for biofuels production; population growth (220,000 people are born each day); the distribution of national wealth in developing economies due to increased income (although accompanied by inaccurate consumption data); urbanization and the creation of mega-cities; government income support programs; high oil prices; production shortages; the devaluation of the US dollar, and speculation by investment funds.

Since we face a new era of growing food consumption, it is not difficult to foresee another crisis. In the past three years, global consumption of wheat has on average grown by 10 million tons per year, corn by almost 30 million tons per year, and soya by 20 million tons per year. Consumption of meat has increased by nearly 20% in the past nine years. In essence, people clearly have sufficient access to food.

---

[11] Published in *China Daily*, 09/02/2011, page 9.

Food prices rose by 40% in one year, and non-food commodities by almost 94%. This has caused inflation, hunger and political disturbances in some developing countries that are net importers of oil and where the population on average spends 30–50% of their incomes on food.

As the G20 leader, French President Nicolas Sarkozy has proposed a strategy for the G20 to lower food prices through increased regulation of commodities markets and the global stockpiling of commodities. We must remember that food chains are highly distorted due to the billions of US dollars spent on subsidies, as well as the existence of high import taxes that have had long-term harmful effects on agriculture export-oriented developing economies. While President Sarkozy is right to worry, we should instead deal directly with the causes of the problem.

In the same chapter, ten solutions were offered that world leaders could use to address the food crisis. These solutions aim to restore equilibrium by rapidly increasing production capacity and efficiency, to the benefit of all parties. These solutions included sustainable horizontal expansion in food production in areas of South America and Africa where water is not scarce; vertical expansion by increasing productivity; reducing food taxes and other barriers that increase prices; investment in global logistics to reduce waste and costs for food transport; using sources for biofuels production that do not compete with food chains; investment to reduce transaction costs in all food chains; creating a new generation of cheaper fertilizers; sustainable supply contracts to farmers for more balanced margins allocation; sharing technological innovations and, finally, education to change consumer habits to avoid loss and even over-consumption of food.

To initiate price controls and stockpiling, as per the current suggestions of President Sarkozy, will make food markets even more artificial. These policies have also been studied by important economists of the OECD, who have shown that such intervention does not work. Other measures such as contingencies of exports and high export taxes may positively control inflation in local markets in the short term, but will ultimately reduce the incentive for farmers to increase production and productivity.

Farmers in various countries have long suffered as a result of production subsidies, which have lowered commodity prices and reduced the incentive to increase production. Instead of subsidies, these farmers require price incentives, access to technology and credit, and market access in order to increase production that will meet the increased demand for food in the next 10–20 years. This is especially true for farmers in developing nations.

The United Nations, FAO and G20 nations should immediately reduce food taxes and provide supplements to lower income groups as a starting platform for the introduction of the abovementioned solutions.

Food production has to be doubled to meet global demand in the next ten years. We should use the available technology, natural resources and human workers to do this, as well as provide incentives for sustainable growth in global food production and trade, thus bringing about the generation of welfare, inclusion and peace.

Chapter 13

Food Chains and Networks Development: A 14 Point List[12]

Every two years, the University of Wageningen/Netherlands hosts the International Conference on Chain and Network Management. With the first conference held in 1996, this May saw the convening of the Eighth Session of the Conference. Around 200 researchers from 40 different countries had three days of discussions on developments in science and the practice of integrated vertical production chains and networks.

This chapter presents some of the important topics discussed at the conference which will be useful for future development. Companies, governments and academics will find this 14-point list useful in identifying areas for future development, emerging topics, and suggestions for policies and regulations. These will contribute to the creation of a more efficient and sustainable food production system in a world of scarce resources.

Chain design, governance and performance — Since chains compete in a global arena against each other and therefore require adequate governance, appropriate contracts can lead to better performance in profit generation and distribution, cost reduction, process management and other aspects, thus adding value to the system.

Waste — An integrated food chain generates waste in most of its processes, and the end products are often wasted as well,

---

[12] Published in *China Daily*, 31/05/2010, page 9.

estimates of such waste running to 40%. Thus, waste management and reduction are of fundamental importance in ensuring sustainability, which is a key demand of today's society. Integrated inventory management and collaborative logistics are among the most important developments for reducing redundancies, waste and depletion of fossil fuels.

Food risks and integrated risk management — There is a need to take an integrated approach to all the risks in food chains, such as contamination and financial risks. Food security should be improved and the costs of this improvement shared with all agents.

Sustainability of chains and certification — Land use, resources conservation, nature and biodiversity should all be taken into consideration. The value, costs and process of certification are also important issues to consider.

Environmental effects on chains and networks — We must consider how the ever increasing effects of an unstable environment are affecting food chains and networks.

Legislation and regulation — Chains are transnational and deal with different governments, laws and institutional environments. Due to constant intervention from these entities, management of chains can often be difficult.

Food and health communication — Chains are now restricted in terms of marketing communications due to society's expectations that they counter over-consumption and obesity through appropriate marketing for children.

Climate change — With higher incidences of droughts, climate unpredictability has resulted in reduced food production and the loss of water and arable land. This leads to the possibility of future climate-related migration.

Information management — Information transparency and sharing has a positive effect on chains' activities by bringing about better management and performance. This also involves the design of information management systems and decision support models.

Table 8: The 14-Point List

14-Point List	Major Developments Needed for the Future
Chain design, governance and performance	• Adequate governance • Contracts should add value • Profit generation and distribution • Cost reduction
Waste	• Waste management and reduction • Integrated inventory management and collaborative logistics
Food risks and integrated risk management	• Integrated approach to risks • Improvement of food security, with costs shared among all agents
Sustainability of chains and certification	• Land use, resources conservation, nature and biodiversity • Review of costs, value and process of certification
Environmental effects on chains and networks	• Understand the effects of an unstable environment on food chains and networks
Legislation and regulation	• Need to deal with different governments and laws • Need to deal with different institutional environments
Food and health communication	• Know what restrictions that chains are starting to face in terms of marketing communications
Climate change	• Measures to counter loss of production, land, crops and water through climate change
Information management	• Development of information management systems and decision support models
Biomass based chains	• Resolve the competition for resources • Growth in the use of biomass and grains to produce energy and fuel
Metropolitan agriculture chains	• Growth of food production in metropolitan spaces
Chain and network intermediaries	• Create a process to map and redesign chains • Ensure such a process adds value to the system

(Continued)

Table 8: (*Continued*)

14-Point List	Major Developments Needed for the Future
Entrepreneurship and innovation	• Agenda for future work
Inclusion and social innovation	• To promote the inclusion of smallholders

Source: Author.

Biomass based chains — With the increased utilization of biomass and grains in the production of energy and fuel, there is pressure due to different chains competing for resources.

Metropolitan agriculture chains — The growth of food production in metropolitan spaces and areas and its integration with modern supply chains should be examined.

Chain and network intermediaries — In the current environment of business giants and lower margins, the mapping and design process of chains does not allow for intermediaries that have no value to the system. Such intermediaries are rapidly being excluded from such processes.

Entrepreneurship and innovation — This was discussed with China Daily readers in my two earlier articles, with the intention of providing suggestions for future work.

Inclusion and social innovation — The capacity of chains to promote the inclusion of smallholders should also be examined.

Table 8 illustrates the 14 points mentioned above. The graphical representation of 14 points can be seen in Figure 6.

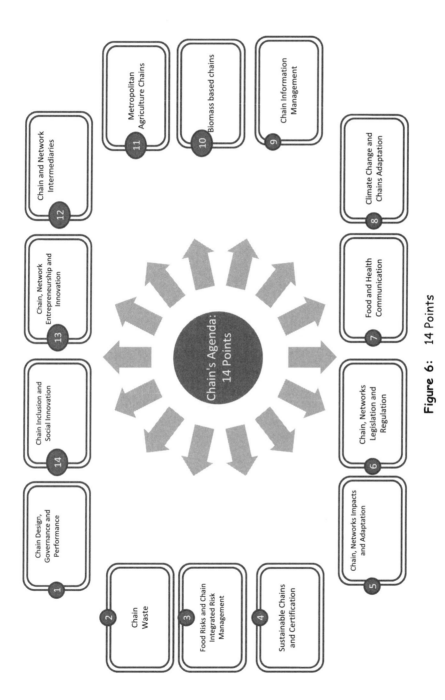

Figure 6: 14 Points

Chapter 14

HOW TO BUILD A STRATEGIC PLAN FOR FOOD CHAIN: THE CHAIN PLAN METHOD

It is estimated that by 2020, food supply in the world will have to be increased by 50%, although the amount of land and water for agriculture remains restricted. The creation of an efficient logistics system is still a challenge for many countries. It is difficult to predict how the demand for biofuels will change, as this will depend on the evolution of automobiles, levels of consumer and industrial demand, as well as institutional environments and government policy. As such, strategic business planning at the national and international levels is required to deal with all these environmental changes, and opportunities for growth in the food and biofuels production chains should be explored.

In Brazil, it will become increasingly necessary to adopt strategic planning and management processes for its various agribusiness systems. Neves (2007) developed the Chain Plan method for "Strategic Planning and Management of Agribusiness Systems", which has been applied to agribusiness systems in Brazil, Argentina, Uruguay and South Africa, among other countries. Its five stages include the initiative of systems' leaders, the mapping and quantification of the agribusiness system, the formation of a vertical organization, formulation of a plan with strategic projects, and the implementation of the plan.

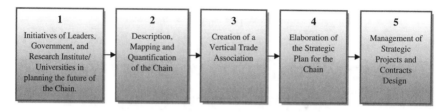

Figure 7: The Chain Plan Method for Strategic Planning and Management of Chains

Source: Neves (2007).

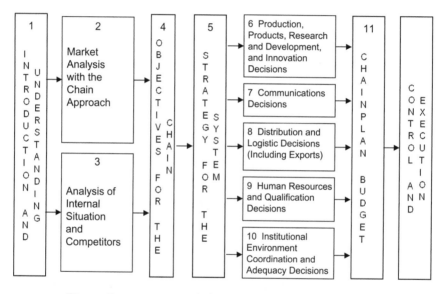

Figure 8: Summary of the Chain Plan Method (Step 4)

Source: Neves (2007).

The Chain Plan method, summarized here in Figure 7, shows a 5-step process aimed at the implementation of strategic planning and management in production chains.

Figure 8 presents the details of Step 4 of the Chain Plan Method. This step is divided into 12 stages to design an integrated strategic plan for the agribusiness system in the following 5 or 10 years.

Each stage is elaborated on in the guidelines presented in Table 9.

Table 9: Guidelines for Demand-Driven Strategic Planning and Management of the Chain

Guidelines for Demand-Driven Strategic Planning and Management of the Chain	
Stage	Necessary Actions
Phase 01 — Introductory	
1 — **Introduction and Understanding**	• To verify if the chain has other plans made and, if so, to study them • To verify the planning method of the chain under study • To verify which teams will take part in the process • To study plans made for production chains in other countries (for benchmarking purposes) • To identify a member of the team who could promote relationships with other chains • In the case of chains with sophisticated planning processes, it must be verified how this model can help the existing model, and how to gradually adapt the previous chain to this one
2 — **International Market and Consumer Analysis with Chain Approach**	• To address threats and identify opportunities from the so-called uncontrollable variables (possible changes in the legal/political, economical and natural, socio-cultural and technological environment) both on the domestic and international markets • To understand existing barriers (tariff and non-tariff) and check collective actions to reduce them • To analyze the final and intermediate (dealers) consumer's behavior and their purchase decision process

(Continued)

71

Table 9: (*Continued*)

Guidelines for Demand-Driven Strategic Planning and Management
of the Chain

Stage	Necessary Actions
	• To analyze opportunities to include goals with regards to the environment, fair trade, sustainability and sustainable development • To analyze opportunities to fit labor institutional environments, both at national and international levels • To set up an Information System to support informed decision-making • To describe the main national and international competitors
3 — **Internal Situation Analysis and Benchmarking of Global Competitors**	• To identify all the strong and weak points of the chain • To map contracts and existing forms of coordination • To describe the existing structures of management and its transaction characteristics • To make an analysis of main competitors • To analyze the value creation, resources and abilities of the chain • To analyze the critical success factors of the chain • To select amongst the chains (not necessarily competitors) where the benchmark for good ideas will be
4 — **Objectives for the Chain**	• To define and quantify the major chain objectives in terms of production, exports, imports, sales to achieve sustainable growth, and to develop solutions for the weak points
5 — **Strategies to Reach Proposed Objectives**	• To list the major strategies and actions that will be used to reach the considered objectives in Stage 4 in terms of positioning, exports, value capture, and market segmentation

(*Continued*)

Table 9:   (*Continued*)

Guidelines for Demand-Driven Strategic Planning and Management
of the Chain

Stage	Necessary Actions
Phase 2 — Plans of Strategic Vectors: Production, Communication, Distribution Channels, Qualification and Coordination (Institutional Adequacy)	
6 — Production, Products, R & D, and Innovations Projects	• To analyze productive potentials and production capacities • To map and plan for production risks (sanitary and others) • To analyze products and product lines, as well as complementary product lines for future expansion • To develop innovation opportunities in the chain, and in the launch of new products • To identify opportunities to settle national and international innovation networks • To foster partnerships with universities and the medical sector • To detail all offerings and potential services • To make decisions related to the joint creation of brands and relevant labels for system use • To analyze and implement the certification process for the chain • To ensure product adequacy with respect to the rules and institutional environment • To ensure environmental sustainability • To make packaging-related decisions (labels, materials, design) • To calculate recurrent investments at this stage
7 — Communication Projects	• To identify the target audience for communications (messages from the production chain)

(*Continued*)

Table 9: *(Continued)*

Guidelines for Demand-Driven Strategic Planning and Management
of the Chain

Stage	Necessary Actions
	• To develop goals for this communication (product knowledge, product reminders, persuasion, among others) and try to define the unique positioning and message that will be generated by the chain • To define the communication tools to be used; that is, define advertising or public relations strategies to boost sales, among others • To make films and international media material that benchmark those already used in other production chains • To review communication actions and determine the annual promotion budget involving all network agents • To indicate how the effectiveness of communications will be measured so that the chain learns more about the best tools to achieve revenue on investments
8 — Logistic and Distribution Projects (Including Exports)	• To analyze the product distribution channels and to search for new ones • To analyze the possibilities of value capture in the distribution channels • To identify possible demands of international dealers and consumers and therefore adjust existing services • To define new ways to penetrate markets (through franchising, joint ventures and other contractual forms, or through vertical integration) • To determine the annual budget for distribution • To verify how distribution can be coordinated with other chains

(Continued)

Table 9: *(Continued)*

Guidelines for Demand-Driven Strategic Planning and Management
of the Chain

Stage	Necessary Actions
9 — **Enabling Decisions in the Productive Chain/Human Resources**	• To conduct training in management for the chain participants • To conduct training in the control of costs and use of technologies • To conduct training in national and international sales • To transmit information from technological centers/research • To conduct training in food production • To offer technical assistance to improve properties • Other appropriate actions
10 — **Institutional Environment Coordination and Adequacy Projects**	• To develop projects to finance the chain • To develop basic infrastructure improvement projects • To develop projects to increase quantity of orders from the government • To develop programmes for isolated productive areas • To push for tax reductions in the production chain • To strengthen export activity through export promotion agencies • To support laws that provide incentives for the use of technologies • To develop a product and product name standardization project • To promote more transparency in legislation referring to projects regarding products and processes • To develop proposals for conflict solutions • To ensure coordination in the development of contracts and proposals

(Continued)

75

Table 9: (*Continued*)

Guidelines for Demand-Driven Strategic Planning and Management
of the Chain

Stage	Necessary Actions
11 — Strategic Projects Consolidation	• All projects generated in Steps 6 to 10 will be consolidated and priorities decided upon
12 — Chain Plan Budget	• Budget for every project, which contains costs and total budget

Source: Author.

Part 2

STRATEGIC PLANNING FOR FOOD COMPANIES

Chapter 15

THE CONSUMER'S KINGDOM[13]

Changes in marketing strategies adopted by companies and the general public perception towards such concepts of marketing have become an exciting area of study over the past 30 years. In this article, we study this process of evolution and then field questions to companies that can be used in their planning processes. We will examine the "wild" view of marketing that was dominant from the 1970s until the 1990s, which then evolved into a new era of consumer sovereignty after an incredible series of macro-environmental changes. Finally, we will discuss the opportunities for companies that aim to satisfy such sophisticated consumers, who are spoiled for choice and have to choose between closely competing companies.

While the "wild" view of marketing is no longer prevalent today, such outdated views still exist in some industries. This "wild" view is held by those who see marketing as the primary means of increasing consumption, through the liberal use of advertising and aggressive selling. New products were designed with the short term goals of sales volume and resultant profits in mind. Marketing was seen as manipulative and companies had a narrow consumer orientation due to a lack of measurement. This problem created an increasing number of problematic relationships. Most companies did not listen to feedback from consumers. Organizational structures were focused around sales, short term results and on-the-spot relationships.

---

[13] Published in *China Daily*, 05/07/2010, page 9.

From the late 1980s to the early 1990s, there were several changes to the business environment in many countries and markets. I consider the most important factors to be the internationalization and deregulation of markets, the rapid rate of technological progress, and the increase in global competition.

Important changes also took place in the sphere of information technology and communications, with the internet and other new technology increasing the speed of socio-cultural changes. Social changes such as the growth of both the consumerist movement and the importance of ethics in social behavior, along with the emergence of the inclusive societal marketing movement, played a crucial role in the last 20 years as well.

These changes brought on a new era of consumer sovereignty, in which production chains were redesigned to satisfy this newly important group of people who were characterised by their professional purchasing behaviour as well as growing expectations. Companies now understood that consumers value their own time, demand freedom of choice, customer welfare and a pleasant experience with rewards. There was also the emergence of consumer ONGs that brought countervailing power against errant firms, as well as increasing public attention towards consumer rights. Risks for errant companies also increased with the speed of communications in the form of discussion groups, Web-based complaints and new media.

Figure 9 shows an overview of the factors that have resulted in the sovereignty of the consumer.

To better explain the figure above, it is important to understand that the sovereignty of consumers led companies to adopt new demand-driven behaviour. This entailed collecting and analyzing information on consumers, competitors and the general business environment, in order to react quickly to environmental changes.

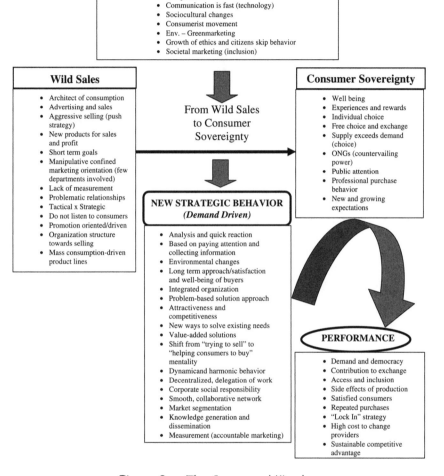

Figure 9: The Consumers' Kingdom

Source: Author.

Companies thus switched to a long range approach that valued customer satisfaction and well being. Such an approach has a new integrated network organization that is both dynamic and harmonic, as well as being decentralized and designed around a

Table 10: Consumer Kingdom — 14 Questions

Consumer Kingdom — 14 Questions
1. How can we collect information about consumers?
2. How can we collect information about our competitors?
3. How can we collect information about the environment?
4. What do we need to do to analyze this information and make quick reactions to environmental changes?
5. How can we adopt a long range approach valuing the satisfaction and well-being of buyers?
6. How do we establish a new integrated network organization that has dynamics and harmony, is decentralized, and includes delegation?
7. How do we formulate a problem-solution based approach?
8. How do we continually search for new ways to solve existing needs by launching value-added solutions?
9. How do we consider and value corporate social responsibility?
10. How can we have a smooth and collaborative network with suppliers, distributors and service providers?
11. How can we have a strong focus on smart market segmentation?
12. How do we promote knowledge generation and dissemination?
13. How do we measure marketing?
14. How do we adopt the "lock in" strategy?

Source: Author.

problem-based solution approach. This new approach works on helping the consumer to make purchases instead of merely pushing products onto them.

There is a continuous search for new ways to solve existing needs. These include launching value-added solutions that consider corporate social responsibility, smooth and collaborative networks with suppliers, distributors and service providers with a strong focus on smart market segmentation, knowledge generation and dissemination as well as accountable marketing.

There are several successful cases of companies with good sales performance contributing to the growth of demand, democracy and inclusion. Such companies adopt the "lock in" strategy, which results in highly satisfied consumers who make repeated purchases from the company. Companies utilizing this strategy build both formal and informal relationships with consumers to consolidate brand loyalty, increase costs for a consumer to switch providers, and establish sustainable competitive advantages with prospects for growth and profitability.

Table 10 shows 14 questions that companies will need to ask themselves when considering plans for improvement.

Chapter 16

DEMAND-DRIVEN ORGANIZATIONS[14]

Consumers nowadays live in an era of choices. We wish to examine the stories of companies and organizations that have done well by making the necessary choices to win over their consumers. Based on sharings from the companies, as well as observations in the ways they behave, we can establish these 10 features of demand-driven organizations.

1 — They listen and pay attention. This is a great characteristic, since to pay attention is difficult. Indeed, it is incredible how in our everyday lives we have to interact with companies that remain closed to feedback.

2 — They do not fear being evaluated. In several organizations we observe a reluctance to establish either formal or informal structures for evaluation, due to the fact that this puts pressure on people.

3 — They dedicate time to think through their work. In the normal frantic business environment, we are often distracted by instant communications that distract us from thinking over what has to be done to meet larger objectives. Technology eases communications between people, but the downside is that we often find our thinking processes disrupted by such communications.

4 — They analyze and then implement macro-environmental changes. They are keen to follow developments in the political, legal, economic, socio-cultural and technological spheres. These

---

[14] Published in *China Daily*, 16/12/2010, page 9.

demand-driven organizations analyze how these trends and movements affect them.

5 — They conduct simulations of possible future scenarios and the likely consequences. This way, they find themselves better prepared for all contingencies.

6 — They connect well with large stakeholders. They utilize several strategies such as maintaining open lines of communication, the establishment of consumer research departments, digital platforms and the empowerment of their front line people. These companies find it easier to establish close connections with stakeholders such as consumers, suppliers, distributors, shareholders, financial institutions and the government.

7 — They believe that they are owned by their customers. They believe that the ability to find out what the consumer wants, and then adjusting the organization to provide it, is what gives the company value in the eyes of the consumer. Believing that this is the case requires a mindset change on the part of employees.

8 — They are not averse to change. In many companies, the staff are indifferent to developments as they believe that nothing will be changed in the long run. This attitude has to be reversed with the thinking that if nothing is expected to change, then first the people must be convinced that they can change things.

9 — In the chapter "Building An Innovative Concept", we explored entrepreneurial behaviour. We see that demand-driven companies always introduce new concepts and solutions into societies.

10 — They also have the discipline to ensure that things happen. They take notes and take actions.

We shall use a simple framework based on three words — the "Fact-Impact-Act" model. Firstly, we list the facts as we know them, from our observations of daily happenings and through the news. Then we analyze the effects of these facts

Table 11: Demand-Driven Organizations — 10 Points

10 Points	Questions	List your Ideas for your Company
1. They listen and pay attention		
2. They don't fear to be evaluated		
3. Dedicate a formal time to think		
4. They analyze and exercise macro environmental changes		
5. Do mental simulations of possible future changes and their impacts, anticipating movements and reactions		
6. High stakeholders touch		
7. Demand driven organizations share a sense that they are owned by the consumer		
8. They don't fear to change		
9. Entrepreneurial and innovation behavior		
10. They also share discipline to make things happen		

Source: Author.

on the organization, both positive and negative. Finally, we decide what to do based on these facts and analyses. Demand-driven organizations are better disposed towards adopting such a framework.

Table 11 shows a working list for managers in organizations. These points could be transformed in questions and shared with management teams and employees, encouraging them to give ideas on how to make improvements to the organization by adopting the 10 features.

Chapter 17

STRATEGIC PLANNING SATELLITE[15]

We present 15 words that represent fundamentally important aspects of contemporary strategic planning and management, each starting with a letter "P", and which combine to form a satellite with the concept of "planning" in the centre. To be better prepared for the uncertain and turbulent future, companies should have this concept of a planning satellite deeply rooted in their systems. Table 12 shows the 15 Ps of strategic planning with appropriate elaborations.

1. Prevision — we must improve our ability to foresee what may happen in the future, such as macro environmental changes and their consequences, before they actually happen. Instead of being surprised, we should be the ones springing surprises on others.

2. Public policies — Public policies and government regulation regarding companies will definitely increase in the coming years. We must use our own associations and organizations to face them.

3. Planet — The growing importance of environment-related issues must be taken into account during planning.

4. People — In the same way, the importance of corporate social responsibility and relations with employees, people inside companies, shareholders and stakeholders will increase.

---

[15] Published in *China Daily*, 02/09/2010, page 9.

Consumers and the press are paying more attention to these subjects nowadays.

5. Productivity — There is pressure to make better use of scarce resources, and to deliver more at even lower costs. Companies have to step up productivity to ensure that this demand is met.

6. Profit — With multiple investment options, the globally connected shareholder will research and compare the profits that can be made from investment. As such, profitability will affect a company's access to credit. This is crucial for planning.

7. Partners — A company is an integrated network, a bundle of contracts, with alliances and joint ventures. We must have the best partners in our business models.

8. Proactiveness — Planning without implementation does not work. Companies must develop a proactive culture where both the institution and the individual are committed to seeing plans through.

9. Providers — There is a permanent need to reorganize supply chains and service providers to be more oriented towards adding value and the inclusion of smallholders. As has already been discussed with *China Daily* readers, inclusion will be one of the most important topics in the future, and companies will be valued by its capacity to promote the inclusion of smallholders.

10. Processes — In planning our activities, we must review all procedures/processes with an eye towards simplification, thus saving time and money.

11. Portfolio — From a marketing point of view, we as companies must offer products and services that are able to adequately solve the customer's problems. Companies should therefore aim to have an adequate and harmonic portfolio of products and businesses.

12. Place — Other than the traditional approach of marketing channels, the places where our products are found

Table 12:   Strategic Planning Satellite

	Questions	List Ideas and Opportunities for the Company
1. Prevision	Ability to see future developments before they actually happen	
2. Public policies	Increasing role of government regulation	
3. Planet	The growing importance of environment-related issues	
4. People	The growing importance of corporate social responsibility and relations with employees	
5. Productivity	Pressure to make better use of scarce resources	
6. Profit	Globally connected shareholders comparing levels of profitability	
7. Partners	A new vision of the company as a integrated network, a bundle of contracts, alliances and joint-ventures	
8. Proactiveness	Renewed company culture determined to take charge of projects to complete them	
9. Providers	A need to reorganize supply chains and service providers towards adding value and smallholders inclusion	
10. Processes	Review all procedures to simplify processes	
11. Portfolio	Offer products, services geared towards solving customers' problems	

(Continued)

Table 12: (*Continued*)

	Questions	List Ideas and Opportunities for the Company
12. Place	Have good points of contact and sales with consumers, promoting convenience	
13. Promotion	Integrated communication activities to have a permanent flow of information with markets	
14. Pricing	To have a integrative and creative pricing strategy to increase both value and consumer satisfaction	
15. Projects	Organize proactiveness and planning in a project-oriented approach to make things happen in a structured way	

Source: Author.

should be hubs where points of contact and sales with consumers can be made, promoting convenience and the exchange of information and experience.

13. Promotion — With the new generation of consumers and new media, planning should consider integrated communication activities in order to ensure a permanent flow of information with markets and consumers, allowing everyone to think fast and react immediately.

14. Pricing — When planning prices, we must have an integrative and creative pricing strategy to add value for the company and its shareholders and consumer satisfaction, with benefits given during the acquisition process.

15. Projects — In any planning process, we need to organize proactiveness and planning into a project management-oriented approach to ensure that things happen in a

Figure 10: Strategic Planning — The 15 Ps

Source: Author.

structured way. Without organized projects, plans and proactiveness, without organized projects, may not contribute to efficiency.

Table 12 summarizes and provides suggestions on how to use these 15 Ps. In each of them, we could ask how are we performing, how we can improve, what are good ideas, and who could be a benchmark. After this step, we can then list ideas and opportunities for the company to undertake. The 15 Ps are graphically represented in Figure 10.

Chapter 18

FOOD COMPANIES' STRATEGIES IN THE NETWORK ERA[16]

All companies must understand that they are not no longer isolated. They operate in a complex network, interacting with suppliers, buyers, consumers, competitors, government and other agents. Companies are bundles of varying types of contracts. The first step for an executive is to describe and draw up this complex network on paper, and then expand it, so that all employees in the company have an overview of its activities, showing that their individual work is not an isolated thing. What happens in the external environment affects the company. If something happens to a buyer or to a supplier, the company is also affected. We must all stay alert, pay attention to our environment, try to foresee changes in the market and plan to meet these contingencies.

Marketing is often seen as a facilitator for transactions that may occur between companies. Companies are becoming more and more interdependent by forming networks with each other. Whenever a company is analyzed we need to construct a network to be used for research, or to work out the methods for segmentation, product differentiation, price determination, setting up of distribution channels and/or communication.

Therefore, the theoretical model of the company network can be defined as the group of suppliers and distributors that

---

[16] Published in *China Daily*, 06/11/2009, page 9.

are participating in related processes. This is called a focus company. These companies participate in the traditional flows of products, services, communication, information, orders and payments necessary to connect the suppliers of raw materials used in production to the consumers of the final products in whatever form they may take.

The concept of networks varies according to the amplitude of "zoom" used, or in other words, the "network of that company". In this sense it is the process of analyzing a company and its group of suppliers and distributors, the existing relations between them and their relation with the environment. It is in essence an interaction- and relationship-centered approach.

What are the advantages of looking at the company as a network?

Instead of seeing the selling company as the proactive party and the purchasing company as the reactive party, the network perspective sees companies as belonging to a network of businesses made of a large number of active and heterogeneous companies. These individual companies interact among themselves and seek solutions for their different problems.

Companies are interdependent on the other members of the network for sales, purchases, information, technology development and mutual access.

Instead of seeing the company as holding all resources, abilities and technology needed to select and develop its strategies, the network perspective infers that no company has all necessary resources, abilities and technology, but depends on its interaction with suppliers, clients, distributors, partners and even competitors for these things. Thus understanding the importance of collective actions and "network zoom" are important for the planning process.

The network of the company being analyzed also allows the addition of facilitator companies, such as freight forwarders, insurance companies, certification companies, warehousing, logistics operators and others. These affect interfaces with other networks, whether by obtaining raw materials or by-products, the inversion of the network (common in cases of recycling or returning via recall, that demand the participation of distributors) or affecting the business environment by introducing variables that cannot be controlled by the company itself (political and legal/institutional, economic, social and cultural, and technological variables).

Furthermore, including competitors in the company's network also allows one to think about collective actions that companies can pursue in marketing, ranging from participation in a sectoral association to creating a joint export venture between competitors. Figure 11 illustrates an example of the design of a company network.

The first component would be the distribution channels that disseminate completed products, and the second would be the company's supply chain, which gathers factor inputs to create products. In other words, these are the systems involved in the supply of all materials that the company needs to produce and sell. This way, marketing considers the part of the cycle that flows between the company to the market. Logically, aspects such as the quality of factor inputs, scarcity, supplier's brands and other aspects related to the company's supply chain have an enormous impact on its marketing, and need to be monitored closely. But other areas such as human resource, finance, production and administration also have an impact on marketing.

Marketing variables are divided into product, communication, distribution and price, with the objective of facilitating both an understanding of marketing in general as well as planning processes. However, marketing actions must be integrated and coherent. Marketing errors happen precisely because of a lack of integration in these tools. It is common to have an exaggerated communication pitch, not corresponding

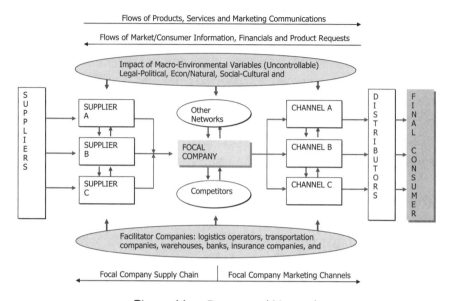

Figure 11: Integrated Network

Source: Elaborated from Neves (2003).

to the true attributes of the product, or a lack of products at the point of sale while putting out a specific advertisement, or even a sales force which is not prepared to offer a product that requires a highly specific set of technical skills to use properly.

In the network illustrated in Figure 11, the role of the marketing professional is to manage the relation between the company and consumer market. There are other professionals in the company who deal with marketing principles and work with supply chain management. In other words, these other people work behind the scenes within the company. Companies need to constantly review their supply chains to reduce costs, buy from the best available sources from all over the globe, and try to find substitute inputs and products while testing for quality and adaptability to ensure that the product fits their criteria. There is a need to establish safe, secure and continuous supply chains in order to minimize inventories, as well as reduce losses due to transport inefficiencies and redundancies, since doing so will also reduce transaction costs. Companies need to rationalize packaging costs and always seek alternatives for constant improvement.

We also list some of the most important strategies for competition in the following years, which can be considered to be the "network era", which are applicable to companies operating in food markets and other markets in the food supply chain.

The first relates to the integrated network approach that has already been discussed earlier in this chapter.

The second strategy relates to supply chain optimization. Companies need to constantly review their supply chains to reduce costs, buy from the best available sources from all over the globe, and try to find substitute inputs and products while testing for quality and adaptability to ensure that the product fits their criteria. There is a need to establish safe, secure and continuous supply chains in order to minimize inventories, as well as reduce losses due to transport inefficiencies and redundancies, since doing so will also reduce transaction costs. Companies need to rationalize packaging costs and always seek alternatives for constant improvement.

In times of compressed margins and global competition, a third bundle of strategies deals with marketing. Companies have to continually review their products to ensure that they are "value-added" for consumers in terms of content, ingredients and packaging. When launching new products, companies should have a clear target, a message that is easy to understand, and do as much research as possible to avoid risks of failure. In today's markets, there is no room whatsoever for new products that end up being failures. Sales of existing products cannot sustain the continued failure of new product launches.

Table 13: Integrated Strategies for Competition

Integrated Strategies for Competition	Important Topics
1. Integrated Network Approach	• Companies are not isolated • They operate in a complex network, interacting with suppliers, buyers, consumers, competitors, government and other agents • What happens in the external environment affects the company
2. Supply Chain Optimization	• Companies need to look at their supply chains to reduce costs • Seek substitute products and ingredients to see if the product fits their criteria • To establish safe, secure and continuous supply chains • Try to minimize inventories and losses due to transport inefficiencies and redundancies • Rationalize packaging costs
3. Marketing	• Companies have to seek to make "value-added" products • Companies should have a clear target when they launch a new product • Have to do as much research as possible to avoid risk of failure • "Simplicity" as the watchword of the new era • Have a very clear consumer focus • Communications (advertisement and others) should be undertaken with a deep understanding of its costs and impacts

Source: Author.

"Simplicity" is also the watchword for marketing in today's world. Companies should simplify market segments, give more attention to income-generating products and have a clear consumer focus. Communications such as advertisements should be done with a deep understanding of its costs and effects. Media exposure is inadvisable without a clear understanding of

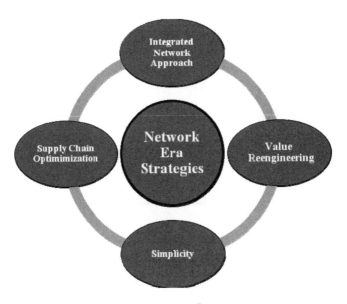

Figure 12: Network Era Strategies

Source: Author.

the return in terms of value that a company is receiving from these investments.

It is a new era in which we must understand the behavior of consumers, and more than this, also understand that the consumer does not want to pay for an inefficient supply chain and wasteful marketing processes. Figure 12 depicts the strategies to be considered in the "Network Era".

Chapter 19

Planning Strategies for 2010–2020[17]

This chapter considers important ideas that are likely to contribute to the shaping of the food industry over the next ten years, affect strategic planning processes and overall positioning strategies of companies, consumers and governments. Table 14 provides a summary of this list of ten points.

Empowerment — Within the next ten years, companies, networks and productive chains will be more valued by consumers if they act to include the base of the pyramid (smallholders) and if they have exercise social responsibility such as ensuring acceptable working conditions. We will also see the growth of fair trade networks. Inclusion will be a topic of growing importance in the following years. Determining how to build sustainable incentives for coordination, such as through associations or cooperatives, will be a central role for governments.

Integration of the economy — A more integrated economy increases the importance of developing countries' supply chains as alternative sources of supply for developed world consumers, and due to this integration, the developing countries' marketing channels are working to sell products to emerging consumers in several countries.

Income distribution — There is a huge internal market growing in several parts of the world, and these emerging consumers

---

[17] Published in *China Daily*, 07/12/2009, page 9.

Table 14: The Top Ten List — 2010 to 2020

10 Major Topics	Research Issues for Managerial Methods and Networks
Empowerment	• Inclusion of the base of pyramid (smallholders) • Social responsibility (working conditions) • Fair trade networks • Margins allocation and distribution
Integration of the Economy	• Developing countries supply chains (trade barriers relief) • Developing countries marketing channels
Income Distribution	• Emerging consumers and positioning of chains and networks • Building incentives for coordination (associations and cooperatives) • Neo-consumption
Climate and Environment (Preservation)	• Low carbon networks • Chains' adaptation to climate change • Renewable energy networks • Measurement and certification of chains and networks • Resource usage efficiency/optimization of by-product utilization • Network reversal (re-use of materials or recyclable inputs)
Technology	• Transparency and information exchange • Consumer-centered "hi-touch" networks • Innovation-driven networks
Merging of Industries	• Nutra-ceutical networks • Nutri-cosmetic networks • Nutri-touristic networks • Nutri-car networks
Risks	• Integrated risk management and mitigation systems • New markets risks (carbon footprint)
Communication	• Use of new means of media communication by chains and networks • Proactive communication with stakeholders • Origin and processes (inclusion) • Traceability

(Continued)

Table 14: *(Continued)*

10 Major Topics	Research Issues for Managerial Methods and Networks
Era of Simplicity	• Management of chains and networks • Market segmentation • New product launching • Customer focus
Network Value Engineering	• Supply chain redesign • Marketing channels being value-added • Collective actions in chains and networks.

Source: Author.

should be more closely studied by companies to determine their positioning. The impact of these new consumers on the planet's capacity to produce adequate food is a major issue.

Climate and environment (conservation) — This topic will gain even more importance in the next ten years, since climate change is a reality. Attention will be focused on the creation of low carbon networks (paying attention to carbon footprints and emissions management), adaptation of networks to climate change, renewable energy networks, environmental certification, resource usage efficiency, network reversal (material reuse and recycling) and network integration for the optimal utilization of byproducts.

Technology — As the drivers of cost reduction, consumers will value network transparency and information exchange and technology systems that will make possible not only hi-tech, but also consumer-centered "hi-touch" networks. Companies and their networks should really be driven by consumers and should therefore communicate with consumers on an individual basis.

Merging of industries — The next ten years will be special due to the merging of industries, like what has happened with mobile phones that now double up as cameras, computers, watches, and more. The world will see the growth of nutra-ceutical networks (food and pharmaceuticals), nutri-cosmetics networks (food and cosmetics), nutri-touristic networks (food and the tourism business), and nutri-car networks (food and biofuels).

Risk management — An integrated network risk management and mitigation system will be of fundamental importance in this connected world. Several risks are present from the global per-spective, ranging from financial crises, plagues and diseases, sustainability and security issues, among others.

Communication — Communication will see major changes, with new media network communication, proactive network communi-cation with stakeholders, associations of origin, communication inclusion processes, traceability and other developments. Communication with the tech-savvy consumer will be a challenge for companies.

Era of simplicity — Simplicity will be valued, in terms of the company's network management, market segmentation, new product launching, brand management, services, costumer focus, sales management, and others.

Network value engineering — We are constantly looking at integrated company networks and promoting permanent supply chain redesign, marketing channels' role in adding value, and consumer intimacy. Permanent evaluations of contracts and building trust in relationships is crucial here.

Part 3

How to Capture Value?

Chapter 20

INNOVATION IN INTEGRATED FOOD CHAINS[18]

A food chain is a complex organization, stretching a long way from input suppliers to farmers, until the final consumer at the end. In the middle, we have farmers, industry, wholesalers, retailers, food services and service providers, like storage companies, transport companies, banks, institutions and organizations. If you think about the orange juice chain, it goes from input suppliers to orange farmers and finally reaches the end consumer. A lot of people, a lot of organizations...

The objective of this chapter is to show how innovation is important to keep a food chain competitive. Nowadays, competition is beyond individual companies, since the competition is between chains. In this chapter, I will start with input suppliers and farmers. These companies have a huge responsibility, since there is increased pressure on the limited resources all over the world.

Inputs play a key role in a food chain. When properly produced and used, they help farmers to get good yields, produce high-quality products and obtain larger revenues, and enable consumers to put safer, tastier and cheaper food on the table. On the other hand, inappropriate production and use management may lead to resource overexploitation,

---

[18] Published in *China Daily*, 19/05/2010, page 9.

negative margins for farmers, and more expensive or unhealthy food for families around the world. Therefore, input management is one of the biggest challenges when it comes to food security.

In order to overcome such problems, researchers from private companies, universities and governments around the world have been seeking innovations in input production and application. Of the major challenges, there are at least 13, as listed in Table 15.

Table 15: Thirteen Major Challenges

Thirteen Major Challenges
1. Development of renewable production inputs that replace non-renewable ones, such as the fertilizers used today. Fertilizers will become a threat to humanity, and we should come up with something to replace them
2. Innovation that allows the reuse of resources and the use of by-products, in order to reduce pollution
3. Innovation that reduces costs for farmers, saving on some operations and improving the farmers' margins
4. Development of new technologies that lead to fewer residual effects from the chemical products used in agriculture
5. Development of more efficient and more economical machinery that saves fuel
6. Development of genetically modified varieties in order to increase yields
7. Innovation towards better grain to protein (animal) and sun to energy (plant) conversion
8. Innovation in biotechnology and natural control in order to use fewer chemical products
9. Innovation that reduces losses in input transport and application
10. Development of genetically modified plants that are more adapted to droughts and water restrictions
11. Development of more efficient feeding technologies for animals
12. Innovation towards the use of more resistant plants
13. Innovation in breeding that leads to precocity, which would shorten the growth cycles and thereby enhance production

Source: Author.

Farmers have demanded many input innovations that would enable them to be more competitive. These are the starting points, but there are several others.

In the last couple of decades world agricultural production has experienced extraordinary improvements, especially regarding yields, cost management and, mostly recently, quality as well. Many of these improvements are a direct result of the ability of farmers to face greater external competition since deregulation, using modern technology and production systems. Nevertheless, there is still a lot to be done in this field, even regarding yields.

The major areas of improvement in which innovation plays an important role are as follows:

✓ Crop and land use decisions that ensure sustainability and resource conservation while making maximum use of the land. Some areas of the world allow three different crops per year.
✓ Development of new crop varieties that present better energy conversion, or are more resistant or precocious, which would reduce the growth cycle and thereby enhance production.
✓ Development of equipment that allows better usage of land, which helps to increase yields.
✓ Water usage, where technologies are developed and applied to reduce consumption.
✓ Development of animal welfare techniques.
✓ Certifications.
✓ Reuse of by-products.
✓ Governance structures, allowing sharing of equipment among neighbors, selling of services, better use of all property assets, in order to be as efficient as possible.

Competition is driven by several factors, one of the most important being innovation. Creating new, effective solutions to problems is the path to profitability and sustainable advantage building for companies. Food production, with all its pressures as discussed in the previous chapters, is an area where financial resources should be applied towards more research that will lead to innovations. In the next chapter, I will discuss innovations needed for the food industry and food distribution.

Chapter 21

Innovation Agenda for the Food Industry and Retailers[19]

In the last chapter, I addressed the fact that a food chain is a complex organization, and showed how innovation is important in keeping a food chain competitive, by discussing the agenda for farmers and input supply companies at the beginning of a chain. Now I will move forward in the chain and discuss the innovation agenda for the food industry and for retailers, in order to attend to demanding consumers. Since the food industry is in close contact with consumers' needs and desires, which have been changing at an ever-faster pace, that is where most innovations are taking place.

Consumers now demand that the industry offer healthier food, food products that enhance beauty and longevity and promote their welfare, as well as products that are more than just products (i.e. convenience, culture, joy, fun). This is illustrated by the concepts of "slow food" and "fun food". The food industry also needs to attend to environmental concerns by promoting product recycling and substitution, fit into the food miles movement, and attend to social concerns by promoting inclusion, wealth distribution and fair trade.

Feeling the pressure for environmentally friendlier, healthier and more distinctive products, the agro-food industry has invested in an extensive agenda of innovation. I would like to list some points that should be in the day-to-day thinking of these companies.

---

[19] Published in *China Daily*, 25/05/2010, page 9.

Developing recyclable and biodegradable packaging materials to address the environmental concerns of buyers is a major point. Consumers don't want to see non-recyclable packaging all over the place. Another point which is being developed more strongly is innovation regarding conservation, for instance in order to increase the shelf life of products and reduce loss (which is over 30% for fruits and vegetables at present).

Flavor improvement is one of the most important parts of research in the industry. There is also a continuous search for innovation in facilitating the storage of products and innovation that leads to the reduction of transportation costs. Food transport is a concern due to losses, costs and the environment.

There is also innovation in the food industry to develop processes that require less water usage and reduce loss and wastage. One way of doing this is through promoting the use of by-products.

New organizational forms are being created by food companies together with pharmaceutical companies and cosmetic companies, in order to innovate in the areas of nutra-ceutics and nutri-cosmetics, thus merging different fields. There is also an increasing regard for business-to-business relationships and innovations in contractual arrangements that benefit the chain as a whole and consequently the consumers.

In addition, much research is dedicated to developing new technologies for industrial optimization and firms are developing new marketing channels, such as door-to-door distribution, outlets and other forms that I will discuss further in a future article.

This is not an exhaustive list of points. But for strategists of the food industry, these points raised definitely should be considered to be on the agenda.

Now we come to the final agent in a chain: the retailer. The retailer is probably the most important participant in a food chain, since it has one of the most valuable assets in the chain: information, due to permanent contact with the final consumer. Super-

Table 16: Innovation Challenges in Production Systems

Inputs	• Renewable sources • Reuse • Cost • Residual effect • Machinery efficiency	• Genetics • Conversion (consumption × production) • Results to the buyer • Better controls (biological)
Production	• Yield per area • Sustainability • Conservation • Precocity • Variety • Water consumption	• Conversion (solar energy) • Resistance • Animal welfare • Certification • Reuse
Agro-industry	• Ecological packaging • Conservation • Flavor • Ease of storage • Lower transportation costs • Lower water consumption • Safety • Loss reduction	• Use of by-products • Nutra-ceutics • Nutri-cosmetics • Relationships • Contracts • Channel optimization (gate-to-gate and others)
Retail	• Offer presentation • Complete solutions • Home meal replacement • Relationship • Purchasing centers	• Express • Delivery • Tasting/trying • Online sales

Consumption	A. Health
	  • Beauty
	  • Longevity
	  • Food on the go
	B. Welfare
	  • Convenience
	  • Culture
	  • Enjoy
	  • Fun food
	  • Slow food
		C. Ecology
		  • Substitution
		  • Recycling
		  • Food miles
		D. Inclusion
		  • People
		  • Wealth distribution
		  • Fair trade

Source: Author.

markets nowadays must promote new buying experiences, such as tasting areas. They should also search continuously for new ways to offer their products, increasing the benefits for consumers.

There is a trend also for supermarkets to offer complete solutions for consumers. The supermarket is becoming a communication tool, a place of knowledge transfer, where consumers learn about the products they eat, and is becoming a place where the industry communicates with its end consumers. Supermarkets are trying to regain some of the market share they have been losing to food services, such as by having a restaurant or selling ready-to-eat food, or what has been called the home meal replacement (HMR) movement.

Supermarkets are also increasing the services provided, with innovation in terms of home delivery, express food, coffee shops and others.

These points, summarized in Table 16, should be considered just as an initial list for food industry and retail strategists to work with.

Chapter 22

CREATIVE PRICING STRATEGIES[20]

One of the most difficult decisions nowadays for companies is pricing, for both products and services. An adequate, sustainable and creative pricing strategy is based on the equilibrium of financial returns desired by companies and the well-being of consumers in the tough global competitive arena.

I work with a framework method that divides this creative pricing strategy (CPS) process into three major phases. The first phase involves understanding the initial value given by the consumer to the product or service. The second is about increasing this value, and finally, the third involves the strategic pricing moves. Let us now look at the first phase.

UNDERSTANDING THE INITIAL VALUE GIVEN BY THE CONSUMER

Before any pricing decision is taken, a company must analyze the external environment: the economic, income and demand conditions (1).

After this, the company should look to the target consumer, understand his behavior, his perception of the reasonable price (using surveys, experts, "food labs"), and carry out initial pricing experiments in different marketing channels. Analyze the total costs for the consumer in buying the product (money needed, time expended, knowledge acquisition, training costs

---

[20] Published in *China Daily*, 27/08/2010, page 9.

and psychological costs) that may be working as "buying barriers". All the consumer's risks in buying the company's product or service should be considered (2).

The third analysis in the first phase of the CPS process is related to competitors, the competing products/solutions and their prices, and how the consumer values and compares the product attributes with that of the competitors (3). To finish this first phase, the company could establish objectives and understand its cost structure with different sales levels.

The analysis of the consumer, competitors and economic environment will facilitate the company's understanding of the value of its product or service in the initial perception of the consumer. After this first phase (understanding) of the CPS framework, comes the second, whereby a company can try to change the initial view the consumer has of its products or services.

INCREASING THE VALUE

The idea is to find and create a unique value position. This can be achieved by reducing the importance of substitutes of the product and comparison possibilities, blinding consumers to the company's competitors (4).

Another way is to measure and communicate the cost of the product as a proportion of the consumer's income or total expenditure (5). The company can also use lock-in strategies, selling the product as a complement to other products established among consumers (6).

It is important to try to communicate the importance of the attributes of the product or service and the problems that may arise if these attributes, for instance quality and safety, are neglected by competitors (7). The company may also consider offering a solution-driven package of products and services to conquer buyers, an approach which is sometimes called bundling (8).

Formulating ways to mitigate the consumer's buying risks found in phase 1 is also an idea (9). Some markets offer the possibility of price skimming strategies for new products or services (offering image, status and exclusivity), capturing value from innovative consumers, first-mover advantage and status-oriented market segments (10).

The last point in the second phase of CPS is to show consumers the economic benefits (like lower production costs) of buying the company's product or service using simple messages and credible commitments (11).

The points raised in the second phase of the CPS framework are strategies to increase the perceived value of the product or service.

STRATEGIC PRICING MOVES

In this phase, the company should be monitoring and anticipating the competition's pricing moves (12), establishing discount policies and promotions, analyzing seasonality and other factors (13), taking an integrated product line approach and looking at their pricing interactions (14), thinking about the pricing adaptations needed when the market faces any macro-environmental (economy) changes (15) and, finally, using web-based strategies, solutions and experiences in pricing (16).

I have used this framework (see Table 17) with some companies, transforming each of these 16 points into questions and answering them with the executives and management of these companies. This can be applied to existing products and services, for new products, and even to help suggest some consumer research and other information-search activities. This is my contribution and I hope it will be useful for readers facing challenges in pricing strategies.

Table 17: Creative Pricing Strategies

Questions	List Your Ideas for Your Company
External environment	
Risks in buying the company's product or service	
Competitors	
Reduce the importance of substitutes of the product	
Compare the cost of the product	
Lock-in strategies	
Communicate the importance of the attributes of the product or service	
Solution-driven	
Mitigate consumer's buying risks	
Price skimming strategies, value capture, first-mover advantage	
Benefits to consumers	
Monitor and anticipate the competition's pricing moves	
Establish discount policies and promotions	
Integrated product line approach	
Price adaptations needed	
Use web-based strategies, solutions and experiences in pricing	

Source: Author.

Chapter 23

Value Capture Trilogy: The Costs[21]

Value capture is one of the most important strategies for companies nowadays. Value capture involves a complete understanding of the network of the analyzed company and a redesign of its activities to increase margins and so capture more value. I call this the "value capture trilogy", since in my understanding we have three major ways of carrying out this strategy. This is a trilogy...

The first of the possible ways of capturing value is by trying to reduce the costs (1) of the company to increase margins and value. Good ideas and creativity are the focus here. The second possibility is via differentiation strategies (2), with activities that will try to increase margins via prices, since the activities increase the value assigned by consumers. Finally, the third bundle of activities relate to collective action (3) that may be performed by the company. This first part of the value capture trilogy will deal with costs.

But how can companies carry out cost reduction to capture larger margins? Basically there are two major components of costs where there are possibilities for improvement: internal costs and costs of inputs and services bought (supply chain costs). I will start with internal costs.

---

[21] Published in *China Daily*, 19/10/2010, page 9.

Here a company should look at all the activities performed and try to see how to improve. These activities are the ones relating to production. The company should explore thoroughly its core competence (a), or what it knows how to do. The second point is how to make better use of its resources and assets (b), analyzing what resources (assets) it has and how these assets could be more used. It is a simple question. We have this asset, how can we use it more and better?

Searching for scale strategies (c) is a third way. What is the production level that will bring scale economies? Examining the quality and cost of materials (d) is another possibility for value capture, by studying new materials and components which may offer better solutions. To have labor efficiency (e) is also important, making the best possible use of human resources and managing overhead costs. Simplicity is the word here.

Continuously redesigning operations (f) towards a "cellular" control of costs is another way. Every activity, like a cell, must be seen and analyzed in terms of how it could be done better. Technology (research and development) (g) and financial architecture (h), looking at the cost of capital and searching for sources of public funding with more competitive rates, complete our list of internal factors that can help the company control costs and capture value.

The second bundle of activities involved in the cost approach of our value capture trilogy (cost, differentiation and collective action) focus on the supply chain of a company (buying processes and relationships with suppliers).

Here a company should try to reduce the bargaining power of suppliers (i), mostly working with strategies related to promoting competition within a group of reliable suppliers and having a continuous trial of substitutes/alternative inputs (even those imported). This would give the company more negotiating power, thus increasing margins. Another possibility is to know the best moments for buying (j), since a supplier has some moments over

Table 18: Sustainable Competitive Advantage and Value Capture Analysis (Costs)

Factor of Evaluation	How to Carry Out?
Explore core competence thoroughly	
Competition among a few reliable suppliers	
Perform operations better than rivals	
Scale economies	
Continuous trial of substitutes/alternative inputs	
Advantage of experience effects	
Reduce bargaining power of suppliers	
Increase company's importance to suppliers	
Quality and cost of materials	
Governance of contracts/reduction of transaction costs	
Efficiency in labor, methods, specialization	
Continuous redesign of operations	
Overhead costs	
Use of assets analysis	

Source: Author.

the year when its demand is lower, and a company with good capital structure can make better purchases at these moments.

Governance of contracts/reduction of transaction costs (k) is also a strategy, since to buy and to negotiate involves other costs (transaction costs) that have an impact on time and other resources of the company. Having good processes that take advantage of information systems and technology will be helpful here.

In this chapter we have listed 11 working points for a company that wants to capture more value in its products and services offered via reducing their costs. These 11 working points may be transformed into opportunity questions (Table 18) to be answered by companies. To continue our "value capture trilogy", the next chapter will explore differentiation strategies, and the following chapter will explore the possibility of collective action towards value capture.

Chapter 24

VALUE CAPTURE TRILOGY: DIFFERENTIATION[22]

To continue our trilogy on value capture, we look at differentiation strategies in this chapter. Value capture involves a complete understanding of the network of the analyzed company and a redesign of activities to increase margins and so capture more value. I call this the "value capture trilogy", since in my understanding we have three major ways of carrying out this strategy. The first major way of capturing value, reducing costs to increase margins and value, was discussed in the previous chapter. The last bundle of activities, which will be discussed in the next chapter, relate to collective action.

How can a company carry out differentiation to capture larger margins? The differentiation approach has five major possibilities, each with its own tools and ideas. The first is the integrated relationship approach, the second deals with products/solutions, the third relates to services/people, the fourth to packaging and the fifth involves brand/image.

In an integrated relationship approach (1), a company should look at intimacy with clients as the first option to be considered. It should establish a so-called lock-in strategy where it creates a complete package for clients that increases the costs of switching to a different offer or company. In such a relationship it is also important to offer performance to the buyer

---

[22] Published in *China Daily*, 02/11/2010, page 9.

(value-driven) as a unique solution that tries to simplify the process and cost of decision making for the buyer.

As for products/solutions (2), in food markets we mostly see products with aggregated nutritional components or attributes, like adding vitamins, minerals or other supplements. Launching innovative products for existing or new and booming markets (e.g. pet food) is another point to be considered. The amount of product in a package is also a strategy, like smaller portions for smaller families or even individual portions. The ready-to-eat market, with products serving complete meals (e.g. rice with beans in the same package), and new market segments (e.g. nutraceutical and nutri-cosmetics) provide chances for value capture.

Another possibility is linked to innovations and products that expand the size of markets. Some companies, when targeting younger generations, offer toys together with food or even other gifts to increase value and consumption. Products that offer ethnic food and new buying experiences face growth in the market. Taking advantage of special occasions (e.g. Christmas, Valentine's Day, the Olympic Games) is another strategy. There is also the growing appeal of the home-made, fresh and locally produced and other connections to be established with consumers. Legal protections, like patents for innovation, are also a strategy for value capture.

Looking at services and people (3), the company should search for a faster, more reliable "just in time" supplier. Another option is to look at the buyer's decision-making process, offering services that may reduce the customer's "fats" in the buying process, by showing the benefits of making this purchase instead of buying from a competitor. In terms of services the company may also try to set a standard for the industry, which works as an entry barrier for competitors. Having the best and most highly trained people gives an advantage in several businesses. All channel-related strategies also have a place here, such as offering locational convenience,

Table 19: Value Capture: Differentiation

	Ideas
Integrated relationship approach	
Products/solutions	
Services and people	
Packaging	
Brand and image	

Source: Author.

point-of-sale presence and new distribution formats for the food-on-the-go segments and other types of buyers.

In terms of packaging (4) there are also several possibilities and techniques, using different materials, beauty, practical, recyclable, transparent, arguments (health and welfare), shelf life, sustainability programs (packaging recycling initiatives), packaging with sounds and smells, to offer supply chain information on packaging (traceability), information on how to use it, of social causes and lifestyles (slim people — fitness).

Finally, looking at brand and image (5) there are well-known strategies for increasing value via improvements to the general brand and image of the company, such as applying the traditional integrated communication strategies to manage its brand and image in the best way possible in order to establish permanent "loyalty contracts" with buyers, receiving added value through the recognition given by consumers to the brand and image.

In this second part of the "value capture trilogy" I have listed five working points for a company that wants to capture more value through differentiation. These five working points may be transformed into several opportunity questions to be answered by companies. To complete the "value capture trilogy", the next chapter will explore the option of collective action.

Table 19 lists the five points discussed in this chapter. You can write down your ideas for the various differentiation strategies.

Chapter 25

VALUE CAPTURE TRILOGY: COLLECTIVE ACTION[23]

In this final part of our trilogy on value capture, let us recall that value capture involves a complete understanding of the network of the analyzed company and a redesign of activities to increase margins and as a consequence capture value. I call this the "value capture trilogy", since we have three major ways of carrying out this strategy. The first way, discussed in the first part, involves reducing costs. The second way is via differentiation strategies, and now, in this chapter, we look at the third bundle of activities related to collective action.

Joint or collective action is defined as a company's activities that could be performed together with another company, or even more than one company. They may be competitors, companies that do not compete but operate in the same markets, or even totally unrelated companies. The possibilities of working together are so huge that they need to be much more explored by companies in the near future due to increasing competition, compressed margins and control costs.

I will divide collective action into seven areas: supply chain (1), internal management (2), products/brands/packaging/ services (3), communications (4), marketing channels and sales (5), pricing (6) and finally horizontal and vertical collective associations (7).

---

[23] Published in *China Daily*, 11/11/2010, page 9.

Starting with joint or collective action within the supply chain (1) (here considered as all the suppliers of the company), the most common activities are related to buying inputs together with other companies in order to increase their bargaining power with suppliers. Another idea is to create a common purchase structure shared with other companies to provide scale gains and reduce redundancies.

With internal management (2) affairs, the ideas include investing in projects with other companies regarding issues related to quality, traceability, information systems, human resources management (sharing training, structures and others), financing and accountancy (using collective tools, sharing accountancy) and lawyers. Here an analysis of what assets the company has, and how these assets can be better used by sharing them with others, is important.

Joint or collective action in products/brands/packaging/ services (3) may also contribute to value capture. Examples include complementing the company's product portfolio with other companies' products, thus offering a more complete package; creating new products and technologies in conjunction (reducing individual investment); facilitating adoption of new technologies and defining a dominant standard; using other companies' brands to enter new markets (brand licensing); sharing services structures for clients, for example those related to the guarantee, maintenance and recall of products; and finally using the same packaging infrastructure.

Joint or collective action in marketing channels and sales (4) could also be carried out to capture value. For example, companies with interests in market segments can share channels and increase sales, or combine efforts to open international markets; salespeople from different companies can complement their product portfolio with products from another company; training on client characteristics (knowledge about client specificities) can be shared, thus dividing the cost among two or more companies; the trade of information among salespeople (sales and potential sales in their markets) can be increased; and joint market studies can be carried out to increase knowledge of territories for definition of the number of salespeople, alignment of territories and determination of quotas.

In pricing (5), several possibilities for joint or collective action are available. One example is to offer a package of products and services with more value and convenience, for instance bundling in agricultural inputs. As a consequence, there is a significant chance that the client's price sensitivity is reduced, thus allowing the company to charge more for the package, in comparison to individual products. Companies also can share discounts (through loyalty cards, for example) and other pricing strategies.

Capturing value through collective action via communications (6) is another way. Examples include conducting joint advertising among companies in the same industry, or companies that have the same target market; joint investments for increasing the consumption of the industry's generic product to create knowledge and form a favorable public opinion of the product so that all participants benefit; sharing public relations infrastructure; sharing stands, common exhibition and demonstration areas and other promotional activities.

The last option for value capture is horizontal and vertical collective associations (7). This includes participation in associations, cooperatives, pools of producers, joint ventures, alliances and other collective forms. The benefits of participating in cooperatives are clear and having strong associations within the industry also supports activities like lobbies, market protection and tax reductions that try to protect margins.

In this final part of the "value capture trilogy" I have listed seven working points (Table 20) for a company that wants to

Table 20: Value Capture: Collective Action

Factor of Evaluation	Ideas
Supply chain	
Internal management	
Products/brands/packaging/services	
Communications	
Marketing channels and sales	
Pricing	
Horizontal and vertical collective associations	

Source: Author.

capture more value through collective action. These seven working points may be transformed into several opportunity questions to be answered by companies thinking up ideas for projects for value capture.

Chapter 26

CREATING A WINNING CONCEPT[24]

A more unstable global environment, lower margins, incredible access to new technologies, huge amounts of information coming from the digital world, higher risks, higher complexity and the emergence of new competitors and "copy-editors" (companies that copy immediately the product) bring a dynamic world of opportunities, challenging our management of companies.

If it is difficult to run a company nowadays, it is even more difficult to have a strategic plan for innovation. Executives suffer from a lack of time, pressure for short-term results, a fast-changing environment that brings "one surprise per day" demanding our attention, difficulties in forecasting and internal cultural problems related to unsuccessful planning experiences from the past and avoidance of more activities. Sometimes planning is difficult since we face the arrogance of those who believe they are the owners of the truth, commonly verbalized as "this doesn't work here..."

The search for success in the current competitive environment requires companies to innovate. A traditional challenge is how to develop an innovation culture supporting the development of new products, guaranteeing growth and profitability. Given this, I think we should move beyond traditional new products. How should we do this?

---

[24] Published in *China Daily*, 23/11/2010, page 9.

Innovations can be even more creative and pursue the objective of creating a concept. I like to analyze examples of companies that launched products or ideas that became concepts. First of all, let me define a concept. It is more than a product; it involves a complete package of solutions, a new behavior, a culture and even a community. It is something new that makes a difference. Imagine as examples Starbucks, McDonalds, or the new digital world: Facebook, Twitter, Google and other innovations that, when they came into the market, introduced a new concept. How to create concepts?

The new product development process has well-known and traditional activities. What I am doing here is adapting them towards a broader inspiration of "concept behavior creation". We may divide the process into seven steps.

1. Proposal of Concept Ideas: Ideas could be raised by consumers in chats, emails, formal letters, discussions, tests, surveys and communities. It involves a description of their problems, suggestions and proposals for improvements. Ideas also could be raised by suppliers, distributors and salespeople, by external and internal research and development programs, employees, shareholders and others. Different parties must be stimulated to provide ideas for concepts, thinking about who should use the concept; what the main benefits are; what the occasion will be; and what needs will be met. The challenge is to talk to consumers, have consumer labs and pay attention.

2. Selection Process for Concept Ideas: This has the objective of reducing the number of ideas for concepts to a few attractive and practical ones, evaluated in accordance with the requirements for success (reputation, brand, R&D, HR, marketing, production, etc.) and the company's competence in the area.

3. Marketing Strategy for Concept: This step plans the size and structure of the concept and looks at the target market

behavior. It plans the positioning of the concept and details such as prices, channels, communications, sales, profit goals in the long term, cost and profit estimates (cash flow Statements).

4. Building the Integrated Concept Network: This phase involves the design of the concept as an integrated network of contracts, participants, the financial plan, partners and others. It is concerned with who will participate in this innovation and what the "architecture" of the concept is.

5. Physical Development and Testing of Concept: This deals with the physical development of the concept, involving all tests and approvals needed. At this moment we should look at how consumers and other stakeholders react and perform market tests.

6. Make it Happen (Launch of the Concept): This phase refers to the go-to-market strategy. We should think in terms of questions such as when (timing choice), where (geographic strategy), to whom (target markets) and how (market penetration strategy).

7. Continuous Redesign: A concept, when created, does not last forever and must be constantly renewed. A concept must bring value to the consumer's time, ambience, build a lock-in strategy (e.g. try to create difficulties for the consumer in

Table 21: Concept Creation

Seven Steps: Concept Creation
1. Proposal of concept ideas
2. Selection process for concept ideas
3. Marketing strategy for concept
4. Building the integrated concept network
5. Physical development and testing of concept
6. Make it happen (launch of the concept)
7. Continuous redesign

Source: Author.

135

changing to a competitor, have clubs and communities like frequent-flyer programs and store cards), communicate clearly, provide superior value in quality and design and be solution-driven. The company must always think about how the concept can be improved.

In this chapter I have suggested seven steps for concept creation. The most important behavior that we should pursue is to pay attention, to be curious and to navigate since good concepts are being created all over the world, one per day.

Chapter 27

CONSUMER RISK ANALYSIS[25]

Do companies have contracts with consumers? First of all, contracts are relationships, and are either formal (written and signed) or informal, like oral contracts based on trust, which have a higher value in many societies than formal written agreements.

The difference between the consumer's expectations and what is received when a product is purchased (dissonance or gap) is something well studied in marketing. Companies face an era of high expectations and these bring extra responsibility. Most companies would like to have loyal consumers who buy what is offered and provide returns. But how can this be achieved? How can these contracts be established?

A traditional analysis could be done here, saying that companies should have a good quality product, a good price, good services, good communication, and an effective marketing channel and sales process. But we can also take a different path, which involves studying risks and looking at the product on offer through the consumer's lens.

Through this lens, companies can look at things from a different perspective and analyze the possible risks that consumers avoid when buying something, starting a relationship or building a sustainable contract. What are these risks? How should companies modify their strategies to avoid them? Here is a list of 10 questions companies should consider.

---

[25] Published in *China Daily*, 11/03/2011, page 9.

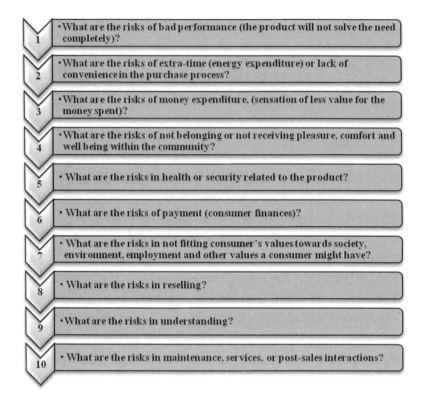

1. What are the risks of bad performance (i.e. the product will not solve the need completely)? It is important to understand what the consumer thinks in terms of quality, conformity and other criteria used to measure performance. Some companies show the economic benefits of using the product on offer, in the case of new technologies, and this is an idea.

2. What are the risks of spending extra time (energy expenditure) or experiencing inconvenience in the purchasing process? Consumers need simple buying experiences, so all the processes as seen by consumers (buying on credit, delivery, showrooms, and internet shopping, among others) should be mapped and analyzed to see how they can be

simplified and sped up. Losing time nowadays is almost a crime!

3. What are the risks of money expenditure (the feeling of getting less value for the money spent)? It is important to understand what value the consumer is placing on the offer and what really is being offered. If there is a gap, probably the company has made a mistake in its advertising or other marketing activity.

4. What are the risks of not belonging or not having pleasure, comfort and well-being within the community? Some products are purchased based on opinions, and will be used in situations where consumers will face the opinions of friends, family, neighbors, colleagues and others. Consumers seek acceptance and sometimes buy a product or service due to a wish to belong, to be part of something.

5. What are the risks to health or security in using the product? If it is a food or beverage, how is the health risk seen, and what is valued in terms of certifications and other associations?

6. What are the risks of making payment (consumer finances)? Will the consumer be able to pay? If not, how can this problem be solved to facilitate payment (e.g. by offering credit)?

7. What are the risks in not fitting the consumer's values regarding society, environment, employment and other values a consumer might have? Production, marketing and other processes should take into account what consumers value.

8. What are the risks in reselling? We can imagine here the case of durable goods that are used and then sold (e.g. cars).

9. What are the risks in understanding? These risks are sometimes neglected. In most markets, consumers want simple solutions, or products that are easy to use and to understand.

10. What are the risks involved in maintenance, servicing or post-sales interactions? These are costs related to insurance, maintenance, the inputs needed, energy consumption and other variables.

Successful consumer relationships nowadays focus on experiences. Being successful in this equation means performing better than the competition in avoiding consumer risks and delivering benefits.

This will create a relationship with consumers, who tend to be loyal if companies keep searching for a better value equation. If the consumer perceives any comprise then the company will be surprised with his new contract with a competitor. This is the risk companies face.

This consumer risk analysis may bring positive results and ideas. The suggestion here, as in other chapters and methods proposed, is to use this list of 10 questions in focus groups with

Figure 13:   Consumer Risks Satellite

consumers and also within the company, gathering the knowledge of sales and marketing people as well as other specialists in order to reduce risks. The consumer will then have a sustainable contract and a profitable relationship with the company, with mutual benefits.

Figure 13 presents a graphical representation of consumer risks.

Part 4

INTERNATIONAL INVESTMENTS AND ROLE OF GOVERNMENTS

· ·

Chapter 28

A STRATEGY FOR INTERNATIONAL INVESTMENTS[26]

So far, this book has conceptually addressed the topic of international investments twice. The first time was to evaluate the capacity of international investments to promote development and the role of government and institutions. Then I went on to discuss how international investments could be promoted and regulated. I will now return to this topic and raise some other points to complement the earlier chapters. Here I have four objectives: (1) to raise the good and bad aspects, (2) to address the need for a national/regional strategy, (3) to emphasize the need for companies to search the world for opportunities and (4) to address the role of governments.

There is still a debate as to whether receiving international investments is good or not for a particular country or region. We should not advocate for one side or the other, but gather all points of view and then do an analysis. International investments do have positive aspects, as discussed in previous chapters, if they promote development by bringing access to international markets and expanding the country's capacity to export, creating jobs and generating taxes for governments, bringing knowledge to a country, bringing credit, and giving confidence, among other things, to the country. If a country

---

[26] Published in *China Daily*, 06/05/2010, page 9.

receives an international investment from a world-class company, that is an endorsement for development and it also serves as a signal to other investors.

The major objections that I have received from opponents of international investment are linked to expatriation of resources from countries, exploitation and exhaustion of these resources and exclusion of future generations of that country from using the resources, sending profits away from local economies and bringing cultural shocks and cultural changes to local communities. Others fear the damage to competition in a country, due to the global capacity of a multinational company that can even promote dumping in local markets, offset by good results in other countries, in order to destroy the local competition. This may lead to the exclusion of local companies in the long term. There are also some nationalist feelings that only products produced in the country, by a local company, are good for the local society. These points should be considered.

But in my view, with a good strategy and a good regulation system, a country can try to avoid these pitfalls and maximize the benefits of these investments. The first step for any country and government would be to have a good strategy, a strategic plan for the country looking 10 to 20 years ahead, which does not seem to be very common in the thinking of governments. With a good strategy it is possible to attract companies linked to the potential of the region, companies with expertise, guaranteed demand (international contracts), clean production systems, high technology (biotech/nanotech) and also companies which guarantee that units of research and development and part of their headquarters will be based in the country receiving the investment.

Let me at this point give the example of Brazil, a country that is witnessing huge inflows of international investment, major economic growth and income distribution, putting pressure on infrastructure, and booming internal markets. Brazil will also host two major events that companies could take advantage of: the Soccer World Cup in 2014 and the Olympic Games in 2016. A good strategy would be to attract international investment and companies that immediately fit the conditions of the country and its opportunities. Just to list some ideas, these could be Spanish, American, Asian and other chains (like Melia, Hilton, Sheraton, Shangri-La) bringing and expanding their networks of hotels (business), investments in entertainment (arenas, parks, museums), companies wanting to produce energy and infrastructure logistics (roads, trains, airports and duties), airline companies participating (now allowed to make up part of 49% of local companies' shares) since it is one of the fastest growing markets, investments in construction in order to build second homes for retired Europeans on beaches in northeast Brazil where there is constant summer (a six-hour flight from Europe), and investments in universities, a booming sector due to the demand for education. There is also room for investments in food, like from New Zealand milk farmers wanting to expand globally, Belgian chocolate companies, Australian/Uruguayan sheep farmers and slaughterhouses.

But all countries and their respective governments, when going to international markets to attract investments, should do their homework, or have the basics of the basics. Such basics include a economy that is working well (growth, low inflation, low interest rates, internal demand), good human resources and talents, reasonable infrastructure to be competitive, security, reasonable taxes and financial systems, attempts to streamline administrative procedures (getting rid of bureaucracy, which is most of the time associated with corruption). A country also has to offer basic resources (e.g. energy, land, water), good suppliers and distributors, and institutions (e.g. judiciary system) that are trustworthy and

Table 22: A Strategy for International Investments

Objectives	Strategies
1. Raise the good and bad aspects	
2. Address the need for a national/ region strategy	
3. Emphasize the need for companies to seek the world for opportunities	
4. The role of government	

Source: Author.

able to speedily resolve problems and disputes. If governments do their homework, together with a good strategy, good regulation systems and a lack of bureaucracy will create the right environment for international investments to come in and promote sustainable development.

Chapter 29

HOW TO EVALUATE THE CAPACITY OF INTERNATIONAL INVESTMENTS TO PROMOTE ECONOMIC DEVELOPMENT?[27]

In this chapter I want to talk about the importance of receiving international investments for all nations, but mostly for developing nations, and try to point out a gap in the usual analysis. What gap is this?

Local or federal governments and other institutions sometimes have difficulties in evaluating the capacity of an international investment to promote economic development. This can also make it difficult for governments to define specific benefits to be derived from such international investor companies, or to convince the local community of those benefits for developing the region, moving the economy forward, generating jobs and exports, among others.

When a transnational company (TNC) comes to a country, it normally comes with several types of resources, not only financial ones. These resources make up our basic list to be analyzed. I want to categorize these resources into six groups in order to assist governments in evaluating international investments in a country. The better the investor can perform in terms of these groups of resources, the better these investments will be. This is based on several discussions I had in 2009 in Geneva, while working on an UNCTAD/ONU project. The groups of resources

---

[27] Published in *China Daily*, 21/02/2010, page 9.

listed here are different, however, since we look also at the local supply chain of a company. If a company can build a good, integrated supply chain, there is a greater possibility for more economic development. Let's move on to the six topics, each with their own sub-topics. It will help you to understand this if you imagine an international food industry investing in a new country.

1. Financial Investments and Expertise: Here we may consider the amount of money that will be invested, and in connection with this, whether the company can provide capital, can open credit lines giving the needed guarantees to suppliers (for instance, local farmers), can gain access to government official credit, has knowledge of credit operations and bureaucracy, has access to international credit and can generate a good reputation for the region and the country. We should also look at its capacity for generating the benefits of foreign currency through increased exports and, finally, the amount of employment generated.

2. Capacity to Provide Technical Assistance: Normally, a TNC has a "how to do package" for its suppliers, helps with farm support, supports sustainability policies and sustainable practices, participates in research and development activities, provides support to achieve standards (ISO, etc.) and transfers skills that will promote economic development.

3. Sourcing of Input Supplies for Farmers: This TNC food company can help farmers by providing them with up-to-date seeds, machinery, genetics, fertilizers and chemicals, thus helping them to produce using the most recent technology.

4. Management Assistance and Service Provision: Here we should evaluate the capacity for assistance with economical/financial controls for farmers and suppliers, training and farming management, transportation and storage, communication skills and certification. Provision of help to local communities with support for demands on public investments in logistics and infrastructure for that country or region should also be considered.

Table 23: Impact of TNCs on Local Community

Resources of TNCs	Impact on Local Community
Financial investments and expertise	• Providing investments (capital) • Opening credit lines, giving the needed guarantees to farmers • Access to government official credit • Knowledge of credit operations and bureaucracy • Access to international credit • Inward investments contribute to the reputation of the region and the country • Foreign currency generation through the increase of exports • Employment generation
Input supply to farmers	• Seeds • Machinery • Genetics • Fertilizers and chemicals
Technical assistance	• "How to do package" • On-farm support • Support of sustainability policies and sustainable practices • Execution of research and development • Support of standards (ISO, etc.) • Transferring of skills • Supply of higher-quality products within the internal market
Management assistance and service provision	• Assistance in economical/financial controls • Training and farming management • Transportation and storage • Communication • Certification • Results/profit of the farm • Support to demands on public investments in logistics and infrastructure

(*Continued*)

Table 23: (*Continued*)

Resources of TNCs	Impact on Local Community
Market access	• Arranging sales contracts
	• Providing access to marketing channels
	• Access to niche markets, e.g. organic, fair trade
	• Providing information on market trends, helping farmers decide what to grow, and enabling reduction on price volatility
Farmers' organizations	• Establishment of local organizations
	• Stimulating the arrangement of cooperatives
	• Building networks of local producers
	• Providing incentives for cooperation

Source: Author.

5. Capacity to Provide Market Access: This is one of the most important points. A TNC can arrange international sales contracts, provide access to marketing channels and access to niche markets (e.g. organic or fair trade), provide information on market trends, help farmers decide what to grow, and enable price volatility to be reduced through long-term contracts.

6. Farmers' and Suppliers' Organizations: This is the last point, one not usually considered or evaluated. I think a TNC should also be evaluated by its capacity to help farmers or suppliers in building what is called "countervailing power", to reduce power imbalances in modern food production chains, although this may seem like nonsense. This can be done by stimulating the establishment of local organizations, stimulating the arrangement of cooperatives, building networks of local producers and providing incentives for cooperation. It is not easy, but I consider inclusion to be one of the most important words for the next 10 years!

Figure 14: Impact of TNCs on Local Community

Finally, studies on TNCs' involvement in food, agribusiness and agriculture are of fundamental importance. Food production needs to be enhanced and in order to accomplish this international investments are needed. At a time when countries are establishing policies regarding food security, with governmental and private funds being allocated to buy land abroad and secure food supply, the role of TNCs increases in importance. There are several lessons to be learned for developing nations trying to attract international investments in agriculture, industry or other areas. Table 23 summarizes the potential impact of TNCs on local communities. In the next chapter, I will look at another important list of topics for government to consider: in which areas and what are the policies and regulations needed to face these international investments?

Table 23 is graphically represented in Figure 14.

Chapter 30

HOW TO PROMOTE AND REGULATE INTERNATIONAL INVESTMENTS?[28]

There is much known about the possible benefits of international investments in an economy. In this chapter, I will point out that an institutional arrangement must be built for a country wanting to receive international investments, since they may have both positive and negative impacts. It is important to have certain regulations in place to try to avoid the negative impacts of transnational companies' investments, and to enhance the positive effects of these foreign direct investments (Figure 15).

There are eight major topics that should be studied and covered by public policies. The objective here is to facilitate local, state or even federal governments and agencies in setting up a framework where international investments can be attracted to promote development and to avoid possible negative externalities.

The first relates to the governance structure of investments. In this area, we include the wide range of possible investments (joint ventures, vertical integration, franchises), money entrance conditions, investment promotion policies, safeguards for risk protection (invasion, expropriation, fees, etc.) and considerations. It must be considered how the direct investment will take place, what sort of asset ownership (land,

---

[28] Published in *China Daily*, 10/03/2010, page 9.

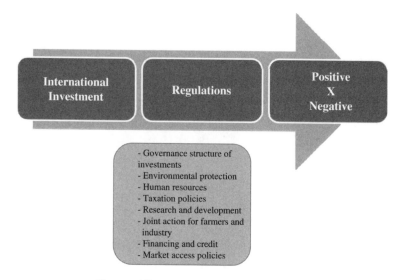

Figure 15: International Investments

Source: Author.

industry and others) is needed, how the stimulus package for these investments (e.g. energy supply, logistics and other related infrastructure) will be built, and even how to remove existing obstacles to attract potential investments.

The second topic relates to environmental protection, which focuses on water use policies, agricultural practices (e.g. soil conservation, harvesting), policies on pollution control, sanitary measures, international standards and required certifications and, finally, policies regarding the conservation of and rights over the country's biodiversity. Some companies have been accused of not having the same environmental practices they have at home, and this should be avoided by means of suitable policies.

The third topic deals with the regulation of human resources. These regulations may cover such issues as salaries, wages, benefits, working conditions, corporate social responsibility, ethics and codes of conduct and community relations. This is one of the most important topics, since most of the previous problems with international investments were related to bad management of human resources.

Taxation policies (taxes) make up the fourth issue which must be defined for transnational investments. Questions regarding the structure of taxes and tax policies, export tax policies, purchase and compensation taxes and possible temporary government tax incentives for the investment to be made, or to be stimulated, are the focus of the analysis here.

The fifth question is related to research and development policies. At this point, the most relevant policies would act as a kind of stimulus to develop local knowledge and R&D. Property rights, licensing contracts and royalties must be discussed. A stimulus for forming linkages with local research organizations and institutions could be an important incentive to integrate and promote development.

The sixth topic is more related to agricultural or agribusiness investments, and deals with joint action for farmers and industry. It is important to have policies stimulating linkages between international investments and local organizations; acting as incentives for forming and sustaining cooperatives and associations; preparing farmers, co-ops or organizations for their relationships with the international investors; and acting as incentives for building sustainable supply contracts. It could be important also to establish a framework for dispute mechanisms and even private arbitration.

The seventh topic relates to financing and credit. It is important to discuss and implement policies that will enable international investors to have access to public sources of financing, state banks and public credit lines. This offer of credit, linked to the technology of the international investor, gives a good possibility of growth.

Finally, the last topic relates to policies regarding market access. These policies can include suggestions for incentives to

Table 24: Suggestions for Public Policies Regarding Foreign Investments in Agribusiness

	Suggestions for Public Policies and Incentives for International Investments in Agribusiness
Governance structure	• How direct investment will take place and types of asset ownership (land, industry and others) • Entrance conditions for resources (money flows) • What the promotion policies for FDI will be • What the safeguards for the protection against risks (invasion, expropriation, fees, etc) will be • What the stimulus package for investments (energy, logistics and other related infrastructure) will be and how to remove obstacles to attract investments
Environmental protection	• Policies on water use • Policies on agricultural practices (soil conservation, harvesting, among others) • International standards and certifications that will be required • Policies on pollution control • Sanitary policies • Policies on conservation and rights over biodiversity
Human resources	• Rural labor & wages • Working conditions • Benefits • Community relations • Child labor • Corporate social responsibility • Ethics and codes of conduct • International labor
Taxation	• Structure and tax policies • Export and tax policies • Purchase and compensation taxes • Temporary tax incentives

(Continued)

Table 24: (*Continued*)

	Suggestions for Public Policies and Incentives for International Investments in Agribusiness
R&D	• Development of local knowledge and incentives for local development of R&D • Property rights and other protection forms, licensing contracts and royalties • Linkages with local organizations/institutions as an incentive
Joint action for farmers and suppliers under contract	• Linkages to local organizations • Incentives for co-ops/associations formation and sustainability • Prepare farmers/co-ops/organizations for the relationships • Sustainable supply contracts • Dispute mechanisms and private arbitration
Financing and public resources	• Access to public sources of financing • Access to state banks and credit lines
Policies on market access	• Government purchasing policies and access to investors • International agreements for market access • General competition policies • Food safety policies for market access

Source: Author.

promote international investments. Ideas that can be considered include the government purchasing products generated by the investment and facilitating local access to investors, international agreements for market access to improve the export channels of this new entrant and general competition policies. With food investments, it is also important to evaluate and promote food safety policies to facilitate international market access.

Studies on international investments in food production are of fundamental importance. It is well known that food production needs to be enhanced, and to accomplish this international

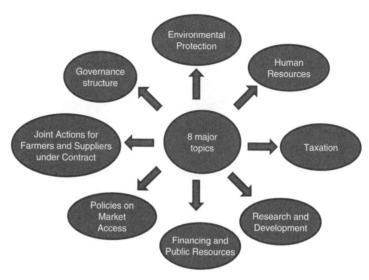

Figure 16: Suggestions for Public Policies Regarding Foreign Investments in Agribusiness

investments are needed. At a time when countries are establishing policies regarding food security, with governmental and private funds being allocated to buy land abroad and secure food supply, the role of these investments increase in importance. This chapter provides governments, agencies and companies involved with international investments with a list of eight major topics (see Table 24) that must be considered for regulation of these investments in order to bring as much sustainable economic development as possible.

Table 24 is graphically represented in Figure 16.

Chapter 31

COLOMBIA: AN EXAMPLE OF THE ROLE OF GOVERNMENTS[29]

In the last few years we started receiving good news from several sources about the turnaround that the country and its major cities were going through. I heard about the wonderful geography and got a taste of the enthusiasm of the Colombian people while interacting with and teaching exchange students from EAFIT University, Medellín, who were studying at the University of São Paulo in Brazil.

Colombia has just emerged from an eight-year government that started the process of returning the country to organized society after decades of difficulties. The major efforts were related to security, with a strong battle against crime. In parallel with these efforts were efficient government management, organization and building of strong institutions, attraction of international investments, promotion of business associations, discussion forums and efforts to improve exports via building bilateral agreements with important markets. From a country that people had feared to visit, it is now becoming a touristic country.

A study was carried out to discover the competences of each region, coming up with differentiated regional policies and agencies for development, with particular attention paid to the

---

[29] Published in *China Daily*, 05/07/2010, page 9.

articulation of the agents. This was done to promote competitiveness based on the traditional cluster approach (bundles of integrated companies with a regional delimitation). The government also worked with investments in education and efforts to attract Colombian talents back to the country. Colombian coffee is one of the most beautiful examples, with the coordination of farmers, investments in promotion and in marketing channels, among other things.

Based on presentations by the government, a second wave of development is now needed. How can innovation be carried out? According to their 2032 plan, Colombia is focused on building world-class businesses, with regional commissions on competitiveness. The new government, elected with almost 70% of the votes, promised to continue the strong and dynamic economic development, with social policies that would allow generation of opportunities and inclusion, since there is a lot to be done with millions of people still in poverty, exclusion, violence and drugs. It is a constant battle.

It is a pleasure to talk to Colombians. Medellín is a happy city, a city with hope. I can feel this when speaking with taxi drivers, who are always a wonderful source of information and have terrible stories from the past to tell.

One exciting sight in Medellín is the Metro system (see Figure 17). There is a "Metro culture" here that makes this public facility an institution, admired, respected and protected by the community. You can find music there, it is clean, and the stations have libraries and other sources of entertainment. This is not a common sight in less developed nations.

There is one Metro line that runs north to south, since the city is a valley surrounded by high mountains to the east and west. In some parts of this line, there is the Metrocable (see Figure 18), a system of cable cars that links the Metro line to the top of the mountains which are full of slums (called "comunas"), integrating these forgotten regions into the city. Places

Figure 17: Medellín Metro

Figure 18: Medellín Metrocable

that would have taken a person one hour to reach by walking up the mountain, after working all day, now can be reached in 10 to 15 minutes by cable car. There are some stations along the line, where people can get in and out. Libraries, cultural centers, leisure/sport facilities, playgrounds for kids were built in these poor communities and the public investments have led to the individual efforts of people to make life better, improving the houses and the surroundings, fostering a sense of citizenship and inclusion. It is a place to be visited, one of the most beautiful inclusion initiatives that I have seen.

Governments have the important role of bringing economic growth, income generation and distribution, geographical equilibrium and access to opportunities. Promoting a favorable environment for the development of clusters is one possibility, enhancing coordination, improving innovation and technological transfer, reducing the lack of trust among agents and promoting exports and access to markets. Visiting Medellín and the rest of Colombia provides an injection of hope that we can change, even in the most difficult situations.

Chapter 32

INCORPORATING SMALLHOLDERS INTO MODERN FOOD CHAINS[30]

Earlier in this book I referred to the importance of including smallholders and small companies in modern integrated food chains, in order to promote development and income distribution. In this article, I want to discuss four dimensions that are important for reaching this objective of inclusion, based on the experiences in Brazil.

The first dimension is that of project management. All projects must have strict criteria in terms of viability and attractiveness. A rigorous analysis has to look first at the technical feasibility of the activities one intends to attract to a specific region. For instance, food processing requires different models for estimating the agricultural and industrial investments and costs. It is also extremely important to analyze the market conditions for the product to be produced. It is clearly a mistake to insist on producing and industrializing products with many competitors when there is no clear regional competitive advantage. It is important to understand demand behavior, quantitatively and qualitatively. All investments today must be accompanied by very strong, world-class project analysis, even more so if they are supported by federal or local governments.

---

[30] Published in *China Daily*, 13/10/2009, page 9.

The second dimension that affects sustainable regional development is integration. In fact, this is the most relevant factor. Many investments fail because they lack a holistic view that considers chain coordination and integration. A firm must buy competitively from suppliers and sell to distributors and end consumers. The way the firm manages relationships with these agents is fundamental to its development. These relationships may range from vertical integration to contractual arrangements or spot market agreements. This is the basic thesis of 2009 Economics Nobel Prize winner Oliver Williamson's discussion on the boundaries of the firm. In regional development, the government may think of attracting an anchor firm that leads production, with control and knowledge of demand information. Take as an example a juice industry as an anchor company coordinating all regional fruit growers. The challenge will be to coordinate supply transactions with smallholders.

Different governance modes, when seen from a social perspective, have different consequences. Vertical integration (where the anchor industrial company owns farms) creates jobs, salaries, taxes, exports and might transfer knowledge from the firm to the employees by means of training programmers, and where, in fact, employees may become entrepreneurs later on. Buying from large growers based in the region also generates the benefits listed above, except that the technological transfer is quicker due to the fact that there are some independent producers and more employees linked to them. Buying from smallholders and cooperatives may be even better in terms of wealth distribution and development, once there is a large enough number of rural families involved in production activities. Attracting anchor companies helps to increase the growers' capabilities through private knowledge transfer and credit facilitation, since one of the biggest challenges for smallholders is access to credit for financing investments and production. A possible form this might take and a key research agenda is public incentives and advantages for projects that involve the largest number of small producers.

The third dimension is the business dimension. It has to be clear that all the agents have to generate profits above their capital costs. Regarding smallholders, their income must be high enough to keep them motivated and committed to the activity. This is the basis for the long-term orientation of the production chain and for economic sustainability. It is important to mention the need for innovation and quality improvements that any chain has to have, and this could be done by forming linkages with local research centers, universities and technical consultants. All parts of the integrated chain must take a long-term perspective.

The fourth and last dimension for regional sustainable development is sustainability. Sustainability comprises three different components: the environment, economic development, and equal wealth distribution for the participants. It is important to motivate national and international environmental certification processes, because they help prepare the firm

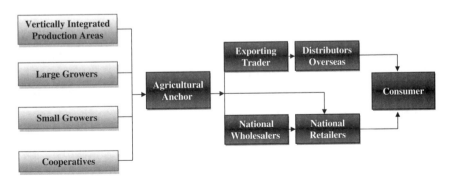

Figure 19: The Integrated and Sustainable Agribusiness Framework
Source: Author.

Table 25: Different Dimensions of Integrating Smallholders into Modern Food Chains

Integration	Sustainability	Business	Project Management
• Inter-organizational • Chain and network perspective • Technological transfer and requested specificities • Cooperatives • Associations • Government participation • Coordinated system • Public banks' participation	• Environmentally friendly • Fair trade • Organic • Job creation • Social development • Regional development • Working conditions	• Profit generation • Cost control • Innovation • Continuous search for competitiveness • Quality refinement	• Rigorous analysis • Rigorous marketing analysis • Organization, scheduling, implementation

Source: Author.

and the region to attend to environmental criteria and later on to open markets. Companies should invest in market segments like organics, fair trade, and promote social inclusion of poor communities.

Sustainable inclusion is the main agenda for the private and public sectors for the next 10 years. This chapter has presented the four dimensions that should be taken into consideration by governments and private companies when thinking in terms of new development projects to promote inclusion that is sustainable, profitable and contributes to growth of the economy, income distribution and wealth (see Figure 19). Table 25 summarizes the different dimensions.

About the Author

Marcos Fava Neves (born in 1968) is Professor of Planning and Strategy at the School of Business (FEARP), University of Sao Paulo, Brazil. He is an international expert on global agribusiness issues. He graduated as an Agronomic Engineer from ESALQ/USP in 1991. He received his Masters of Science in 1995 and PhD in Management (with a special focus on "Demand-Driven Planning and Management") from the FEA/USP School of Economics and Business in 1999. He completed post-graduate studies in European Agribusiness & Marketing in France (1995) and Marketing Channels and Networks in the Netherlands (1998/1999). He lived in the USA in 1977 and 1978 where his first job was that of a paperboy.

He specializes in strategic planning processes for companies and food production chains and is a Board Member of PENSA and other public and private organizations in Brazil. In 2004, he created the Markestrat think tank Group that handles international projects, studies and research in strategic planning and management for more than 40 organizations. He has supervised more than 20 PhD theses and MSc Dissertations. In 2008, he became CEO of the second largest biofuel company in Brazil. Following the boom in agribusiness in Brazil and the emerging position of Brazil in world food business, he gave more than 350 presentations in Brazil and 120 in 15 other countries.

His writings focus mainly on supplying methods for business. He has published 70 articles in international journals and has authored and edited 25 books, published in Brazil, Uruguay, Argentina, South Africa, Netherlands and the USA. He is a regular contributor for the *China Daily* Newspaper, *Folha de São Paulo* in Brazil and has written two case studies for Harvard Business School, in 2009 and 2010. He can be reached at mfaneves@usp.br or favaneves@gmail.com.

EPILOGUE — PEOPLE WHO MAKE IT HAPPEN

I hope that you, the reader, have enjoyed this book. I have shared my opinions about several topics and also some tools that I have used to facilitate planning and comprehension.

Due to several modern developments and their impacts on us, we have to address these issues in order to make progress.

To move forward, we really need to make things happen at both a personal and an organization level. In this epilogue, I will share my views on what constitutes characteristics of managers that "make it happen". These are the ten most relevant areas for professional development.

Be Tuned — Managers need to be linked to what is happening globally in terms of the macro environment, such as developments in politics, economics, the sociocultural sphere and technology. They need to read newspapers, watch news programs, pay attention and listen. In addition, they must travel and have a global view that incorporates cultural sensitivity. Dennis McKnight, a friend from Canada, always tells me, "Stay home, stay stupid."

Be Simple — Learn how to simplify things by being practical, searching for basic and faster solutions to solve any given problems. Reduce costs permanently.

Be Adaptive — Consumers change, competitors change, solutions change. The capacity to adapt in a fast-changing environment is one of the most important characteristics of a modern human.

Be Innovative — Students and managers should be innovative and create their own businesses and solutions by moving away from the basics. Innovation is a search for new ideas that are not readily thought of by most people.

Be an Investor — We are facing global competition, and hence we should never stop studying, progressing and wishing to learn. We cannot be satisfied with where we currently stand. It is our responsibility to invest in ourselves in order to become better professionals.

Be Related — A very important characteristic that we should develop is the capacity to relate with others, build teams, work in groups and share knowledge and solutions. Respect differences and each individual's characteristics, since doing this allows us to have a broader view. Allocate people to jobs that they do best. While we motivate others to be competitive, at the same time we should try to be inclusive and add value to people in the team in order to boost their confidence.

Be Broad — Be prepared to give opinions supported by good arguments, as well as to understand and respect the reasons for differing opinions. One way to improve on this aspect is to read editorials in order to learn to see the facts from different perspectives, thus learning to balance arguments.

Be a Dreamer — Keep dreaming of achieving our targets. Constantly search for more dream objectives to work towards in order to prevent complacency and stagnation.

Be Disciplined and Result-Driven — A manager has to deliver results. Personal discipline is important when managing the overall development of the business and the welfare of the staff. Develop a passion for efficient planning and measurement of results. Be present and available whenever the company needs you to contribute in any way.

Be Communicative — Managers should communicate well. While communication must not be excessive, it should get the job done by constantly addressing the objectives to be met.

Equilibrium and elegance are essential when sharing major achievements with the team.

To conclude, the most undesirable characteristics for young managers are arrogance, a boring style and personality, complacent behavior, and a lack of ethics and character. Selfishness and insincerity are also seen to be undesirable characteristics.

This article can be used by students and professionals as a tool for individual planning. One idea is to ask how you yourself, your boss and your friends can make improvements in each of the ten topics listed. Once you have done this, then "make it happen".

Once again, thank you for reading this book.

Marcos Fava Neves